The Remnant

THE GRADUAL REPLACEMENT OF TRUTH

By

Mel Johnson

Published by Alignment Publishing
Ruskin, Florida

Scripture quotations are from the King James Version of the Bible unless otherwise noted.

Library of Congress Control Number: 2026909557
ISBN: 979-8-9956471-0-2

Printed in the United States of America

To the Most High, whose Spirit led, instructed, and sustained every word of this work. To my parents, Marcus and Fannie Johnson, whose love and support carries me through every season of my life. To my Bride, Arline Azcona-Johnson — my ezer kenegdo (my help meet), my ally, my confidante — whose companionship sustains me, and whose encouragement anchors me in truth and purpose.

If in this life only we have hope in Christ, we are of all men most miserable.

— 1 Corinthians 15:19

CONTENTS

NOTE ON SOURCES

Unless otherwise noted, all Scripture citations are drawn from the King James Version.

The Eth Cepher — from the Hebrew eth, meaning divine, and cepher, meaning book, together conveying divine book — is cited throughout this work for its Hebraic transliterations and its inclusion of texts not found in standard Protestant translations. It is not presented as a replacement for the King James Version but as a supplementary resource where its content bears directly on the arguments developed in this manuscript.

Citations from the Book of Jubilees are drawn from the Eth Cepher translation. Jubilees is not part of the Protestant canon. It is cited throughout this work as an ancient text of historical and covenantal relevance — recognized as scripture within the Ethiopian Orthodox tradition and preserved among the Dead Sea Scrolls — and is included here for its bearing on the theological arguments developed in this manuscript.

INTRODUCTION

Tradition and belief are often used interchangeably, yet they are not the same. Belief requires engagement. It must be examined, reinforced, and lived to mature into conviction. Tradition, however, requires no such participation. It sustains itself through repetition. It is inherited, practiced, and normalized — often without ever being questioned.

Over time, this distinction becomes critical. What is believed can be corrected. What is practiced without examination becomes embedded.

The danger is not always found in outright rejection. More often, it is found in something inserted so gradually it never required scrutiny. Not the removal of what is true — but its quiet replacement.

Replacement does not happen abruptly. It unfolds slowly. What is unfamiliar becomes visible. What is visible becomes acceptable. What is accepted becomes established. Once established, it is rarely challenged.

Eventually, what was once true is no longer recognized — not because it has changed, but because something else has taken its place.

This is the nature of tradition when it is left unexamined. It can shape belief, not through revelation, but through repetition. Over time, what is practiced begins to define what is believed, and what is believed — if not assessed — can drift from the truth it once reflected.

The Bible warns that tradition can render the Word of God ineffective. The issue is not tradition itself, but the authority it is given. When practices passed down through generations are accepted without examination, they can move beyond expression and become substitution — replacing what was revealed with what has merely been repeated.

> *But in vain they do worship me, teaching for doctrines the commandments of men.*
>
> (Matthew 15:9)

This pattern of replacement extends beyond tradition alone. It is also reflected in where trust is placed. As belief in God diminishes, reliance on humanity increases. What was once anchored in the authority of God becomes redirected toward the authority of man.

In this shift, belief itself is redefined. No longer rooted in communion with the Creator, it becomes adaptable, shaped to align with personal preference, cultural acceptance, and human reasoning. A vague acknowledgment of a "higher power" replaces a submitted relationship with the living God. In this way, God is not always rejected; He is reinterpreted, adjusted, and displaced.

As reliance on God weakens, dependence on human authority grows. Leaders (politicians, clergy, intellectuals, and voices of influence) become the interpreters of reality. Their words offer clarity, their systems offer structure, and their conclusions offer comfort. Yet, what provides comfort does not always produce truth.

Trust in human wisdom offers the illusion of control, but it often distances us from divine dependence. Following God requires submission to His authority — an authority that challenges human reasoning, confronts pride, and calls for obedience beyond understanding. Where human wisdom seeks to explain, God calls us to trust.

True growth, therefore, demands more than passive acceptance. It requires discernment. Not only to hear, but to examine. Not only to receive, but to test. Faith must be anchored in what is eternal, not shaped by what is convenient. We do not claim to possess truth; we submit ourselves to it.

This is the pattern revealed in Christ. He did not speak from His own authority but came in the name of the Father. Jesus declared:

> *"I am come in my Father's name, and ye receive me not: if another shall come in his own name, him ye will receive."*
>
> (John 5:43)

Many read John 5:43 as a direct reference to the Antichrist — the one who comes in his *own* name whom the world will receive with open arms. That reception will not be coerced at first. It will be enthusiastic, because he will speak exactly what the itching ears have been waiting to hear.

Paul confirms this in 2 Timothy 4:3-4 — they will heap to themselves teachers, not submit to them. The people choose the voice that validates them.

Christ identifies a tragic irony baked into fallen human nature: the authentic is rejected while the counterfeit is embraced. The reason is not coincidental — it is structural.

> *"For I have not spoken of myself; but the Father which sent me, he gave me a commandment, what I should say, and what I should speak."*
>
> (John 12:49)

Jesus spoke only what the Father instructed, never glorifying Himself, but directing all attention to the Source of truth. His life stands in contrast to the pattern of man — where authority is often self-appointed, and truth is often self-defined.

He asks a question that remains as piercing now as it was then:

> *"How can ye believe, which receive honour one of another, and seek not the honour that cometh from God only?"*
>
> (John 5:44)

At the heart of all scriptural teaching is a charge — one that cannot be delegated or inherited. Each believer must examine what they believe, not through assumption, but through discernment. This discernment does not originate in human intellect, nor is it sustained by collective agreement. The Holy Spirit guides it.

The Holy Spirit does not affirm what is merely familiar. He reveals what is true. He searches, instructs, corrects, and brings into remembrance what has been spoken by God. Where tradition repeats, the Spirit reveals. Where man asserts, the Spirit discerns. Where substitution has occurred, the Spirit restores.

This book is not written to introduce something new. It is written to reveal what has been displaced. It explores the gap between God and humanity, and questions whether our standard of living has, in subtle and often unrecognized ways, replaced God's standard.

It is also written with a clear purpose: to uproot, pull down, destroy, and overthrow any thoughts or ideas that might hold the reader captive, clearing the way for liberated believers to walk in the Spirit of God.

This work requires more than intellectual engagement. Every reader is invited to approach it with an open and surrendered heart — releasing pride, submitting thought, and trusting the Holy Spirit to reveal what the mind alone cannot receive.

Alignment is essential to what follows. Alignment is not an idea to be understood — it is a life to be lived. It is not found in moments, but in consistency. It is not revealed in words, but in response.

Many believers are praying, hoping, and praising their way through life, maintaining a measure of spiritual satisfaction while continually returning to be refueled. Yet something remains unsettled.

There is effort, but not clarity.
Movement, but not direction.

This tension is not always the result of a lack of commitment. It is often the result of misalignment. Scripture makes this plain:

"Can two walk together, except they be agreed?"
(Amos 3:3)

Agreement precedes movement.
Without alignment, there can be no true walk with
God.

The Remnant will examine the patterns that have shaped belief and expose where substitution has occurred, but it will also call for something deeper than understanding. Alignment is lived through response, through obedience, and through agreement with God.

Allow the Holy Spirit to teach and to remind. What is revealed here is given to be received, experienced, and lived. Only then can we come into alignment with what God desires us to know and to see.

It is an examination of patterns that have existed from the beginning, patterns that have repeated throughout history, and continue even now. It is a call to recognize what has been normalized, to examine what has been accepted, and to return to what has been established.

So it is, as the earth groans under the weight of its iniquities, that a faithful remnant stands apart. The heavens bear witness to the turmoil below, yet among the chaos, a light endures — faint, but unyielding. These are those who refuse substitution, who reject imitation, and who return to what is true.

Their path is not without trial. They are evaluated, refined, and pressed, yet they endure — not by the strength of man, but by the Spirit of God. They walk the narrow way, guided not by the voice of the many, but by the Word that does not change.

This is their calling. To remain. To discern. To endure. They are The Remnant. Because truth has not been lost.

It has been replaced.

"the race is not to the swift, nor the battle to the strong, ... but time and chance happeneth to them all... But he that shall endure unto the end, the same shall be saved."

(Ecclesiastes 9:11; Matthew 24:13)

CHAPTER 1 — THE REMNANT

Even so then at this present time also there is a remnant according to the election of grace.

(Romans 11:5)

God has always preserved a remnant — never the majority, never the visible. They remain when faithfulness is no longer convenient. Throughout history, while many have drifted under pressure, others refused to move. Not because they were stronger or more capable, but because they were anchored to something unchanging.

The concept of a remnant is often misunderstood. The word itself suggests something diminished after the majority has been removed: a fragment, a portion, something reduced. Even this definition, though accurate in form, is incomplete in meaning. What appears lesser has consistently been used by God to accomplish what is greater. What seems small is significant, and what appears reduced is not without purpose.

In the context of God, the remnant is not what is discarded — it is what is preserved. Not by chance, but by design — set apart, sustained, and established according to His purpose.

They are not defined by number, but by alignment, the residue of His people, those who cling to the truth that He is, was, and always will be. They are the children of the Most High, called to endure the erosion of God's standard and the resistance of a world that does not recognize it. They remain firm while everything around them shifts, unmoved while the path beneath them bends. They are the enduring flame — often overlooked, yet preserved with intention, set apart to fulfill His purpose.

Throughout Scripture, a pattern emerges, one that does not shift with time, culture, or circumstance. When corruption covered the earth in the days of Noah, preservation was not found among the masses, but within a single family. When Elijah stood under the weight of despair, convinced that truth had vanished and that he alone remained faithful, God revealed what could not be seen: there were still thousands who had not bowed. What appeared to Elijah as isolation was preservation.

This pattern reveals something critical: truth has never depended on the majority. It has never required agreement to remain true. Truth stands independent of acceptance. For this reason, truth often appears isolated — not because it is weak, but because it remains uncompromised.

The majority, by nature, move with influence. They adapt to what is familiar, align with what is affirmed, and shift under pressure. Truth does not. Truth does not adapt. It does not bend. Truth does not evolve to accommodate preference. It remains.

Because it remains, those who align with it will often find themselves moving against everything else. To remain aligned carries a cost. It requires resisting what has been normalized, rejecting what is widely accepted, and standing when it would be easier to adjust.

Yet the greatest threat to the remnant is not always opposition, but subtle replacement.

Truth is rarely discarded outright. It is not often attacked directly. Instead, it is displaced. Something else is introduced as an alternative. It appears reasonable. It appears beneficial. It appears harmless. Eventually, it assumes the place of what was originally established.

God is not denied; He is repositioned. Truth is not rejected; it is reinterpreted. What was once clear becomes obscured — not because it has changed, but because something else has taken its place. Yet, even in this process, something remains.

There are always those who recognize the shift, who sense that what has been accepted does not align with what is true. This recognition is not merely intellectual; it is internal. It disrupts comfort. It challenges what has been normalized. This is where transformation begins. Not in learning something new, but in recognizing that something has been misplaced.

They are those who hear and respond, who see and realign, who recognize and return. They are not immune to pressure, but neither are they governed by it.

They remain, not out of ease, but out of conviction. Not because they are many, but because they are aligned. They stand when others shift. They hold when others release. They are what remains when everything else has been moved. They are the remnant.

A MUSTARD SEED

Repeatedly, God has demonstrated that what appears small is not without power. With five loaves and two fish, thousands were fed. With Gideon and only three hundred men, vast armies were overcome. Through one Son, salvation was extended to the world. The remnant has never relied on number or strength, but on the power of the Spirit of the living God. The Scriptures speak plainly:

> *"...though the number of the children of Israel be*
> *as the sand of the sea, a remnant shall be saved."*
>
> (Romans 9:27)

This has always been the pattern, and it remains so. As the disciples once stood in admiration of the Temple, Jesus redirected their focus — not to what was seen, but to what was coming. He spoke of deception, of wars, of division, of famine, of unrest. He described a world unraveling under the weight of its own departure from truth. Yet this was not the end. They were only the beginning of sorrows. In such a time, many would falter. Trust would erode. False teachings would rise, offering answers while leading many astray. The world would not appear to be falling — it would appear to be advancing.

Yet, there would remain those who endure — those who do not turn away but draw nearer; those who walk by faith and not by sight. They are steadfast and overlooked, often dismissed, yet unmoved.

There is a call — quiet, yet persistent, unmistakably resonating within the hearts of God's people. It is both familiar and unsettling, as though something long buried is being brought to the surface. It confronts identity. It exposes distance. It awakens remembrance.

Through the Holy Spirit, there is a restoring, a revealing of what has been obscured. A reminder of who they are: children of God, heirs of promise, called not to remain where they are, but to return. This return is not merely physical, it is inward. It is the renewing of the mind. It is the realignment of the soul. It is the decision to leave what has been accepted and return to what is true.

God prepares His people through His Word. Through the instruction of the Holy Spirit, they are cleansed, strengthened, and equipped, not for a moment, but for a walk. Still, many will hear and walk away, believing they have already received enough.

THE FEAST

Around the world, dinner serves as a cherished moment of togetherness, a familiar rhythm woven into the fabric of daily life. On a Saturday evening, the air is filled with the aroma of dishes carefully prepared by the loving hands of family members, infused with cultural spices, and served with tender kindness. Loved ones gather with eager anticipation, memories of past meals shaping their expectations of another satisfying feast, a ritual that consistently fills the stomach and gratifies the senses.

The experience begins with the aroma: subtle, inviting, drawing each person closer. Eyes scan the table, taking in what has been prepared. Collard greens, cornbread, and an array of carefully crafted dishes come into view. Oxtails, rice, and green beans are set alongside desserts: caramel flan, apple pie, pineapple upside-down cake. Brownies, fruit, and iced cold sweet tea complete the spread. A pause for prayer introduces stillness, a moment of gratitude before participation.

Yet even within this shared experience, not all approach the table the same way. Some engage fully — tasting, savoring, responding with appreciation. Others measure their portions carefully, taking only what they feel is sufficient. Some hesitate, mindful of their limits, thinking ahead to what remains for later. Then there are those who dismiss what is left altogether — unwilling to return to what has already been received.

Not everyone views what remains in the same light. For some, what is left behind has no value. For others, time deepens its richness. What was prepared once revealed something new when revisited, its flavors more pronounced, its depth more apparent. In this, a pattern emerges.

God's people have been blessed with rich spiritual nourishment: truth that satisfies, bread that sustains. Many receive and engage in the moment — they depart content. Yet often, what has been given is treated as the whole feast rather than the first course. The assumption is made that what was heard once does not require revisiting. Familiarity can do that; it dulls expectation. What was once remarkable becomes routine. But God does not become ordinary. What He gives does not diminish with repetition — it deepens. What was good reveals itself as greater. What satisfied once satisfies more fully when returned to. It unfolds, deepens, and reveals more to those who remain.

So, while many move on, a few stay. They return, not out of routine, but out of perception. They know there is more than what was first understood. They make time. They prepare. They wait on what God continues to reveal.

The invitation remains open. All are called — yet not all return. Many, convinced they have received enough, turn away — unaware of what has been prepared beyond what they have already tasted. But some remain. They return not because they are different in nature, but because they are different in response. They stay positioned. They endure.

And through those who remain, God will reveal what has yet to be realized — for no eye has seen, no ear has heard, and no mind has conceived what He has prepared for those who love Him. This is the pattern of the remnant. What is left is not without value. What is overlooked is not without purpose — it is preserved with intention. God has never treated what remains as insignificant. He has consistently revealed that what is left behind is often what is preserved.

Just as Christ, the cornerstone, was rejected and cast aside, yet became the foundation of redemption — so too does the remnant reflect this pattern. What the world dismisses, God establishes. What is overlooked, God preserves. The remnant is not what was discarded. It is what remains — set apart, sustained, and prepared for His purpose.

Are You His Remnant?

CHAPTER 2 — A PEOPLE DEFINED BY ALIGNMENT

For they are not all Israel, which are of Israel.

(Romans 9:6)

God has always had a people. Not a people defined by location, language, or outward identity, but a people defined by covenant faithfulness. From the beginning, God's relationship with man has not been determined by proximity, but by covenant. It has never been enough to exist near what is true; one must be aligned with the truth. This distinction, though subtle, is foundational.

Many have lived among God's people without ever becoming part of them. Others have been scattered across nations, removed from what once defined them, yet remained connected by something deeper than geography. The difference between the two is not found in association, but in response.

To belong to God is not to claim Him — it is to respond to Him. This truth is often misunderstood. The declaration that God has a people can sometimes be interpreted as exclusive, suggesting that specific groups are included based on visible acts of devotion, while others are left without clarity or context. It can appear as though belonging is reserved for a select few, reinforcing one group's standing while excluding others entirely. But this perception is incomplete.

God is the Creator of all living beings, culminating in the creation of humanity. He breathed the breath of life into man, granting him consciousness and free will. In the beginning, man knew only God and His commands, living in harmony with the Creator. There was no division, no competing influence — only alignment. Until sin arrived, and with it, everything began to change.

As knowledge expanded and influences grew, choices multiplied. Mankind began to act independently of the One who created and fathered them, stepping away from the original relationship God intended. What was once alignment became separation, not by force, but by decision.

Humanity, in this state, mirrors the prodigal son — leaving the comfort and stability of the Father's presence in pursuit of self-defined fulfillment in an unfamiliar world. Yet even in departure, God did not abandon His creation. The Father set in motion a plan of redemption, not to compel return, but to make it possible. The choice to leave was ours. The choice to return remains ours.

There are standards in God's family — clear, recognizable, and purposeful. They are neither hidden nor insurmountable. While many are familiar with the Ten Commandments, Jesus revealed their foundation when He said:

> *"…Thou shalt love the Lord thy God with all thy*
> *heart, and with all thy soul, and with all thy mind.*
> *This is the first and great commandment … Thou*
> *shalt love thy neighbour as thyself."*
>
> (Matthew 22:37–39)

These are not merely instructions — they define identity. They capture the essence of what it means to belong to God. Those who resist the urge to lean on their own understanding, and instead respond to Him, are received by a Father who rejoices in their return. He is God and Father to all who choose to serve Him. Regardless of the categories created to divide humanity, God has a people, and all humanity may become His people.

> *"... God our Saviour, Who will have all men to be saved, and to come unto the knowledge of the truth."*
>
> (1 Timothy 2:3-4)

God has always had a people — never defined by where they are, but by how they respond to Him.

RACE, ETHNICITY AND MISIDENTIFICATION

Humanity has attempted to define what God has not. Race has been used as a measure of identity. Yet in Scripture, physical characteristics are descriptive — not determinative:

> *"I am black, but comely..."*
>
> (Song of Solomon 1:5)

This is description — not identity.

Identity makes a claim about nature; description makes a claim about appearance. Race, as is understood today, is a construct formed not by divine design, but by human classification. The concept of race as a formal system of categorizing humanity emerged during the so-called Enlightenment period, when thinkers such as Linnaeus and Blumenbach divided people into groups based on physical features, assigning value and hierarchy where God had established none. What followed was not discovery; it was distortion.

Race evolved into a framework used to divide humanity based solely on outward appearance. It reduced entire groups to superficial traits, assigning meaning, value, and identity based on skin color and skull size. Over time, it overshadowed what once defined culture: history, tradition, and faith, and replaced them with a system rooted in external observation rather than internal truth.

It is an invented ideology lacking biological foundation, yet it has been used to separate, classify, exalt, and degrade. Its influence extended into politics, professions, financial systems, and social order. Through each, it falsely attributed intelligence, worth, and superiority based on appearance alone. Race, therefore, cannot determine who God has already defined. It should never be used to identify His people.

Ethnicity, however, presents a different consideration. Ethnicity is defined not by outward appearance alone, but by shared culture, history, lineage, customs, and lived experience. It reflects continuity — something passed down, preserved, and recognized across generations. In this sense, ethnicity may carry weight, not as a measure of superiority, but as a reflection of origin and identity within history. Scripture reveals that God established a people:

> *"For thou hast confirmed to thyself thy people Israel to be a people unto thee for ever: and thou, LORD, art become their God"*
>
> (2 Samuel 7:24)

This declaration is specific. God set apart a people — Israel, not based on physical appearance, but through covenant, lineage, and relationship. Yet even here, care is required. Ethnicity alone does not define covenant standing. While it may reflect origin, it does not guarantee belonging.

Just as race cannot determine who belongs to God, ethnicity, though more grounded in history, cannot establish identity apart from covenant. It may point to a people, but it does not replace the requirement of response.

This is where distinction must be made: Race is a construct imposed from the outside. Ethnicity reflects continuity preserved from within. Neither, on their own, determines who God's people are.

> **Ethnicity** — marks origin and heritage. It is inherited, not chosen. A Hebrew is a Hebrew by descent.
> **Covenant** — marks relationship and responsibility. It is entered, not inherited. Even those born into the lineage had to respond to what God established.
> **Alignment** — marks ongoing faithfulness. It is lived, not declared. The remnant is not defined by where they came from — but by how they respond to God.

God's people are not identified by what is seen, but by what is aligned. So, even with the establishment of Israel, a deeper question remains: Who is Israel?

LINEAGE

Scripture traces identity with precision, and the idea of a people's lineage tracing back to a single individual is consistently established throughout the Bible. The suffix *ites* signifies descent;

it identifies a group of people traced back to a progenitor. It is not merely a label; it is a marker of origin.

From Shem came the Shemites. Shem, one of Noah's three sons, was among those through whom the earth was repopulated after the flood:

> *"These are the families of the sons of Noah — Shem, Ham, and Japheth — and by these were the nations divided in the earth after the flood."*
>
> (Genesis 10:32)

From Eber, a descendant of Shem, came the Hebrews, those connected not only by lineage, but by identity within a developing people. From Abraham came Isaac, and from Isaac came Jacob, whose name was changed to Israel:

> *"And he said, Thy name shall be called no more Jacob, but Israel..."*
>
> (Genesis 32:28)

From Israel came a nation — the Israelites. From Judah, Israel's fourth son, came the Jews. The word Jew itself is derived from Judahite, signifying those who descended from Judah.

In this way, Scripture reveals a clear pattern: lineage establishes origin. It tells us where a people come from. It does not complete identity. God created all people; lineage alone cannot determine who belongs to Him. It may identify a people historically, but it does not define their standing before God.

A people may be traced by blood, named by ancestry, and recognized by descent, yet still exist outside of alignment with the One from whom all life comes. Lineage, therefore, is a beginning —not a conclusion.

LANGUAGE AND SEPARATION

Understanding the difference between language and speech is essential when considering the development of humanity and the emergence of God's people.

Language is broader than speech. It is not limited to words alone; it includes expression through symbols, gestures, signs, and shared meaning. Speech, by contrast, is the verbal expression of language — the use of the voice to communicate what is understood internally.

For example, two individuals may not share the same spoken words, yet still communicate effectively through gestures, expressions, or symbols. A raised hand can signal pause. A nod can communicate agreement. A written sign can convey direction. These are all forms of language, even when speech is absent.

Conversely, speech without shared language can fail. Two people may speak to one another, yet if they do not share meaning behind the words, communication breaks down. The sound is present, but understanding is not.

From the beginning, God created all things after their kind: land, vegetation, living creatures, and humanity. He gave man dominion over His creation and the responsibility to cultivate and steward it. In that early state, humanity functioned in unity, not only in purpose, but in communication.

> *"And the whole earth was of one language, **and** of one speech."*
>
> (Genesis 11:1)

This unity extended beyond words. It reflected shared understanding, shared culture, and shared expression. The people were not divided by interpretation, background, or identity. They were aligned, not only in communication, but in experience. Language, in this sense, was more than communication; it was continuity — but that unity did not remain.

As humanity progressed, alignment shifted. What was once unified began to diverge. Language, which had been given as a gift of communion, became the instrument of division. In Genesis 11:1-9, God intervened, not by removing speech, but by altering understanding. He confused their language, disrupting their ability to communicate effectively with one another. What followed was separation.

People were scattered across the earth. Distinct languages emerged. Cultures developed. Customs formed. What was once one became many. Nations were established not only geographically, but culturally and linguistically.

Language became tied to identity. It began to reflect belonging, marking groups by shared expression, shared meaning, and shared experience. Within this newly divided world, God called Abram, not because he was already set apart, but because he would be.

From among many nations, from within a scattered humanity, God began to establish a people — not defined by language alone, but by covenant. The Hebrew people would emerge within this landscape, distinct not because they were isolated from the world, but because they were called out from it.

THE COVENANT

God entered covenant with Abram, choosing him from among the people of the earth. He said to him:

> *"I will make thee exceeding fruitful, and I will make nations of thee, and kings shall come out of thee. And I will establish my covenant between me and thee and thy seed after thee in their generations for an everlasting covenant, to be a God unto thee, and to thy seed after thee. And I will*

give unto thee, and to thy seed after thee, the land wherein thou art a stranger, all the land of Canaan, for an everlasting possession; and I will be their God."

(Genesis 17:6–8)

When God spoke these words, Abram already had a son. Ishmael had been born through Hagar — the result of human reasoning applied to a divine promise. They did not wait on God. They moved ahead of Him. But the covenant was never meant to follow human initiative. God made that clear. What man produces cannot carry what God purposes. The covenant would come through what He Himself would give — in His time, by His means, on His terms. Ishmael was blessed, multiplied, and made into a great nation, but he was not the carrier of the covenant promise:

"And as for Ishmael, I have heard thee: Behold, I have blessed him... But my covenant will I establish with Isaac, which Sarah shall bear unto thee at this set time in the next year."

(Genesis 17:20–21)

The distinction was intentional. God's covenant would continue through Isaac, the son of promise, conceived not through human intervention, but through divine fulfillment. Through Isaac came Jacob. Through Jacob, Israel. Through Israel came a people established not merely to exist, but to reflect God.

This covenant, though established through a people, was never meant to expire in them. It pointed beyond them toward fulfillment through one:

"Now to Abraham and his seed were the promises made. He saith not, And to seeds, as of many; but as of one, And to thy seed, which is Christ."

(Galatians 3:16)

The covenant, therefore, was not only generational, but it was also directional. It moved from promise to people to fulfillment.

Promise preceded people. People preceded fulfillment. Each stage carried what came before it and pointed to what was still coming.

The children of Israel through this line were the first to be both Hebrews by lineage and Israelites by covenant identity. From among the Hebrews, God chose Israel. From among Israel, He chose Judah, through whom the promise would continue and the Messiah would come. This separation was not accidental. It was intentional. God set apart a people from among all people, not to isolate them, but to sanctify them. As it is written:

> *"Behold, I will separate unto myself a people from among all the peoples… and they shall be my people and I will be their Elohiym (God)."*
> (Jubilees 2:20, Eth Cepher)

This calling was carried forward through Moses, a Hebrew and an Israelite, a descendant of Levi, who was sent to lead the children of Israel out of Egypt and into the land God had promised.

As a Levite, Moses stood within the tribe set apart by God for priestly service — the same tribe through which the priesthood of Israel would be established.

In the wilderness, this covenant relationship was established more fully. God gave His laws, statutes, and judgments, speaking through Moses, who would declare and preserve them among the people. During this time, the children of Israel were not only delivered; they were also defined. Moses declared:

(Deuteronomy 26:16–17)

There were commands to follow and consequences to consider. This marked a new phase in the covenant relationship, one that required not only belonging — but obedience. After impressing upon them the weight of this responsibility, Moses, along with the priests and elders, spoke plainly:

(Deuteronomy 27:9)

They became His people through covenant but remained His people through obedience. God's people, therefore, are the children of Israel and their descendants — those whom He separated and sanctified unto Himself. Yet even in this, understanding must be clear. They are not identified by physical characteristics. They are not confined to national origin. They are not recognized by shared language alone. God's people are identified by what they reflect.

The covenant was never meant to produce a stagnant people defined by exclusion. It was meant to cultivate a people marked by transformation — growing, expanding, and expressing the attributes of God in such a way that their identity would not be known by appearance, but by the fruit they produce.

THE ISRAELITES

God's covenant extended through Abraham's lineage and into generations to follow. From this covenant line a people began to take shape. These were not simply descendants of a man — but the early formation of a people defined by both origin and calling.

From among the scattered nations, the Abrahamic line was distinguished — not by outward appearance, but by divine selection. Within this lineage, a structure began to emerge. Families became tribes, and tribes became a people with shared identity and purpose.

Among these tribes, one would carry a unique role. From within the broader body, a specific line was set apart through which a greater promise would unfold. This was not a matter of preference, but of design — each part contributing to something that extended beyond the immediate generation.

This people did not emerge fully formed. They were developed over time, through movement, hardship, and transition. Their identity was not simply inherited; it was shaped. They were God's Newborn.

Under the leadership of Moses, they were brought out of bondage and into a process of transformation. What began as deliverance became formation. Removed from one system, they were being prepared for another.

In unfamiliar terrain, their dependence on God was tested. Their understanding was challenged. What was once known was no longer sufficient for where they were being led. This was not only a physical journey, but an internal one. They were learning what it meant to function as a people set apart. Instruction became central. Order was introduced. What was once practiced without structure now required order. Their development required more than memory; it required participation. This process revealed something essential: Identity is not sustained by origin alone.

The Israelites, therefore, were not simply a people who came from somewhere; they were a people being shaped into something. Their distinction was not found in how they appeared, but in what they were being formed to reflect.

GRAFTED IN

To graft is to transplant — to take what was once separate and join it into something living, for the purpose of union and growth.

Birth established origin. It did not determine belonging. Those from other nations who aligned themselves with God's ways were always received among His people. They were not guests. They were not exceptions. They were grafted in — brought near not by bloodline, but by response to what God had established.

> *"And when a stranger shall sojourn with thee, and will keep the passover to the LORD, let all his males be circumcised, and then let him come near and keep it; and he shall be as one that is born in the land..."*

> (Exodus 12:48)

This was not symbolic — it was functional. The stranger who chose to walk according to God's commands was no longer treated as separate, but as one within the covenant. The same laws applied:

> *"...for whosoever eateth that which is leavened, even that soul shall be cut off from the*

*congregation of Israel, whether he be a stranger,
or born in the land."*

(Exodus 12:19)

The Hebrews were among many peoples within God's family — distinct in their calling, but not exclusive in His reach.

Not every person was a Hebrew. Not every Hebrew was an Israelite. Not every Israelite was a Jew.

(See Appendix B — Lexical Study: Simon, Peter, Rock, and Cephas for further study on how names carry covenant significance.)

Yet even among these distinctions, there were those who walked with God who did not share the same lineage. What unified them was not birth, but transformation. God's acceptance was not merely legal — it was spiritual. The stranger who aligned with God was not only counted among the people but became part of them in identity and expectation. They were grafted in.

This pattern did not begin and end at the borders of Israel. It continued through every stage of God's dealing with humanity. Ruth, a Moabite woman, chose to remain with Naomi and declared:

"...thy people shall be my people, and thy God my God."

(Ruth 1:16)

She was not born into the covenant. She entered it through response. She was received, honored, and placed within the lineage through which the Messiah would come. What determined her standing was not her origin — it was her alignment. This is the consistent pattern. From the wilderness to the land, from the land to the diaspora, God's reach was never confined to bloodline. Those who turned toward Him were received. Those who turned away — regardless of lineage — were not.

In Egypt, God identified His people not simply by lineage, but by those who were under His covering, those who suffered, endured, and were set apart among others:

> *"...I have surely seen the affliction of my people which are in Egypt..."*
>
> (Exodus 3:7)

Israel was distinct. Not isolated — identified. Called to live among nations without being shaped by them. Within their own number was a mixed multitude — people from other nations who aligned themselves with God's ways and were counted as part of His people.

These distinctions were never meant to divide. Identifying categories are not barriers. They are mirrors. Jew and Gentile. Believer and unbeliever. Each one reflects a response — to align or to turn away. Judah gave the name. Israel gave the identity. But neither lineage nor label completed belonging. Only response did. The door was never closed. It remains open.

Joining God's people required more than association — it required transformation. Those who were grafted in aligned themselves with what God had established. They entered a structure — its laws, observances, its community — and accepted its requirements. They chose to become what they were not by birth — God's people. This pattern did not end with the Old Covenant—under the New Covenant it was revealed more fully. No longer is belonging defined by outward observance or works of the Law, but by inward transformation.

(Romans 2:28–29)

Through Christ, access is extended fully — not by heritage, not by performance, but by response. Through faith, by grace, through the circumcision of the heart and the leading of the Holy Spirit, all who choose Him are grafted into the Body of Christ. The stranger becomes a son. The outsider becomes family.

So, the one born outside the lineage, yet born of the Spirit, is no less a child of God than one born within it. They were scattered — yet not lost. In that scattering, something was revealed.

*Israel is no longer confined to what is seen, nor by what is
measured.
It is not identified by physical characteristics.
It is not contained within national borders.
It is not recognized by language alone.*

God's people are identified by what they produce. As it is written:

(Matthew 12:33)

Those who violate God's commandments and laws do not reflect His love. It is not enough to say you are God's people — your actions must bear witness to that claim. Israel is not bound to land, nor defined by any present attachment to it. For they were

29

scattered — intentionally, deliberately — according to the will of God.

To reduce Israel to territory is to misunderstand its transformation. Israel was not lost, it was transformed.

CHAPTER 3 — BONDAGE BEYOND CHAINS

*While they promise them liberty, they themselves
are the servants of corruption: for of whom a man
is overcome, of the same is he brought into
bondage."*

(2 Peter 2:19)

MIGRATION

Jacob had twelve sons: Reuben, Simeon, Levi, Judah, Dan, Naphtali, Gad, Asher, Issachar, Zebulun, Joseph, and Benjamin, the youngest.

After selling Joseph into slavery, ten of his brothers deceived their father, convincing him that a wild animal had devoured him. Jacob, presented with Joseph's garment and his brothers' account, believed his son was gone.

In time, a severe famine fell upon the land. As conditions worsened, Jacob kept Benjamin close to him— Joseph's only full brother, and his last remaining son by Rachel. Fearing the loss of his youngest son, he sent his remaining ten sons to Egypt to secure provisions to sustain their household during the famine.

In Egypt, through a series of events orchestrated by God, Joseph had been elevated to a position second only to Pharaoh. What began in betrayal had been transformed into purpose. Joseph, now matured and established in a foreign land, had become instrumental in preserving not only Egypt, but many surrounding nations during the famine.

When his brothers came before him, they did not recognize the man Joseph had become. But Joseph recognized them. What followed was not immediate revelation — it was a process that exposed, assessed, and restored. In time, Joseph revealed himself to his brothers. He reunited with them, and soon after, with his father. Jacob and his entire household of seventy persons were brought into Egypt and settled in the land of Goshen — positioned there by the hand of God. What began as survival became settlement. What began as provision would eventually become bondage.

AFFLICTION, DELIVERANCE AND RESISTANCE

For a time, peace remained in Egypt. After the deaths of Israel, Joseph, and Pharaoh, the land continued in stability until a new king rose to power. This king did not know Joseph. He had no awareness of the Hebrew who once preserved Egypt through years of plenty and famine. What was once remembered as provision was now forgotten, and what was once welcomed was now viewed with suspicion.

What God promised to Abraham was now visible in Egypt — a people multiplying beyond what any system could contain. What the king could not control, he feared. He reasoned that in a time of war, Israel might align with Egypt's enemies. What was once a source of strength was now perceived as a threat. Motivated by fear, the king chose to subjugate them. There was no provocation. No uprising. No cause for hostility. Only fear, and fear became policy. The children of Israel were afflicted, and their labor was made unbearable.

God remembered His people. He heard their cries and moved on their behalf, bringing them out of bondage. They departed as a mixed multitude — not Hebrews alone, but all who were under His covering.

Still, though they were delivered physically, something remained. Their long association with captivity produced a familiarity that, at times, felt safer than trusting God. The years they endured in bondage left a deep and lasting imprint upon their minds. Their thinking was shaped by their experiences. Their responses were formed by what they endured. They learned to depend on systems, not on God.

After leaving Egypt, Pharaoh's army pursued them. As it drew near, fear overtook the people, and they turned against Moses, saying:

> *"...Because there were no graves in Egypt, hast thou taken us away to die in the wilderness? wherefore hast thou dealt thus with us, to carry us forth out of Egypt?"*
>
> (Exodus 14:11–12)

Though they witnessed deliverance, they longed for what was familiar. In the wilderness of Sin, hunger tested them again. Once more, they contended with Moses and Aaron, saying:

> *"...Would to God we had died... in the land of Egypt, when we sat by the flesh pots,* and *when we did eat bread to the full; for ye have brought us forth into this wilderness to kill this whole assembly with hunger."*
>
> (Exodus 16:3)

Their response revealed something deeper than circumstance. God brought them into a place where He alone would be their source and sustainer. Yet they resisted, not because God failed, but because their understanding had not yet been transformed. Their chains were broken, but their conditioning remained.

Bondage did not end when they left Egypt. It lingered in their minds. It shaped how they saw God, and it shaped how they saw themselves. They knew lack, fear, and uncertainty. They were treated as less than human. These experiences shaped their response to the world around them.

What we understand through concepts like epigenetics gives language to this reality: prolonged hardship leaves a lasting imprint, shaping behavior and perception across generations.

In His mercy, God provided manna for the children of Israel in the wilderness — daily sustenance, sufficient for each day. It appeared with the morning frost, meeting their immediate need.

Yet even in provision, they resisted — revealing why God identified Israel as a stiff-necked people.

CHAPTER 4 — THE WEIGHT OF ASSIMILATION

"For as he thinketh in his heart, so is he…"

(Proverbs 23:7)

EFFECTS OF OPPRESSION

Years of oppression left their mark. Prolonged pressure reshapes people. What is endured over time does not remain external; it begins to internalize, producing effects that become both pervasive and normalized.

Under sustained conditioning, a psychological shift can occur in which the oppressed begin to reinterpret their captors. What once was clearly harmful can begin to appear necessary. Over time, captors may be perceived not only as authorities, but as protectors, providers, or even allies. This dynamic is commonly described as Stockholm Syndrome.

***Stockholm Syndrome** — a condition in which individuals develop a psychological alliance with their captors as a survival response during prolonged captivity.*

Its effects do not end when captivity ends. They extend beyond the environment in which they were formed. When a person has adapted to a system long enough, anything that contradicts that system can feel threatening. What is true can feel unfamiliar. What is unfamiliar can feel unsafe. At this point, perception becomes inverted.

What was once understood as freedom begins to resemble instability. What was once known as bondage begins to feel like security. This is the effect of prolonged oppression. It does not merely restrict behavior — it reshapes interpretation. Even after years of immersion in Egyptian practices, values, and ideologies, something remained — remnants of a culture that was not inherently Egyptian. Yet those remnants were no longer sufficient to preserve full identity.

They were removed from their land, their principles, and their way of life. They were being reshaped. What once defined them was being replaced, not abruptly, but gradually. In that process, they became unknowingly beholden to the very system that oppressed them.

ASSIMILATION

Before moving further, a baseline must be established. One must understand, as comprehensively as possible, where we are before we can move toward where God intends us to be. To do this, we must first examine the process of assimilation.

Assimilation does not occur all at once. It is not immediate, nor is it always forced in its later stages. It is a gradual process, subtle, progressive, and often unrecognized. What begins as exposure becomes familiarity. What becomes familiar is accepted. What is accepted is practiced. What is practiced long enough becomes established.

Cultural assimilation may be understood as the process by which a minority group comes to resemble a dominant group. It involves adapting to the culture of another people, eventually reaching a state in which that adaptation becomes normalized.

This definition, however, is incomplete. It describes the process and the result, but it does not account for the forces that have historically imposed assimilation — colonialism, the Inquisition, and other systems that enforced cultural, religious, and linguistic replacement upon a people. This is how systems shape perception — quietly, consistently, and often without recognition.

Throughout history, this pattern is evident. A people placed into environments not originally their own do not immediately reflect what surrounds them. Their language is different. Their customs are different. Their traditions are different. Their understanding is different.

But gradually, exposure produces adaptation. When God's people were brought into bondage, they did not share the language of their captors. They did not share their culture, their traditions, or their religious practices.

Over time, however, what was foreign became familiar. What was unfamiliar became accepted. What was accepted became lived.

A people who once knew who they were began to adopt what was not originally theirs — language, customs, traditions, and systems of belief. Not through immediate rejection of identity, but through gradual exposure and repeated participation.

This understanding serves as a guiding light. God's children live in a world they are not of, practicing traditions that were not originally theirs, influenced by a culture they did not inherit, and speaking a language they were compelled to learn.

Within this condition, there are voices that attempt to minimize what has been lost.

WHAT HAS BEEN LOST

Some will say, "It does not matter when you observe the Sabbath, as long as you honor it." Others will say, "It does not matter what you call God — He knows who you mean." Still others will suggest that identity has already been defined, removing the need for further examination. These perspectives reflect the effect of assimilation.

Though historical events brought God's people into foreign environments, it is assimilation that has shaped how they now identify themselves within them.

What has taken place is not random. It is a systematic process — methodical, sustained, and effective. It has influenced how value is measured, how success is pursued, and how identity is perceived. What is pursued often appears attainable yet remains just beyond reach — like a moving target that cannot be secured.

> *The appearance is convincing. The substance is not.*

This is not rooted in assumption — it is rooted in revelation. It is through seeking God that understanding is restored, revealing who we are and who we were before prolonged separation, before generational disconnection, and before the loss of knowledge of The Most High.

ASSIMILATION THROUGH CULTURE

> *Culture shapes what is lived. Tradition preserves what is repeated.*

Culture is broad. It forms patterns, beliefs, behaviors, and values over time. It influences how people think, how they act, and how they understand the world around them.

Tradition is more specific. It is what is passed down, what is practiced, what is repeated until it becomes familiar.

Tradition lives inside culture.

Gradually, what is repeated begins to feel natural even when it is not aligned. This is assimilation. It is not sudden, but gradual. Not through rejection, but through adoption.

What is observed repeatedly becomes normalized, and what is normalized begins to define behavior. Over time, what was once external is no longer recognized as influence; it is perceived as identity. Assimilation does not require agreement. It requires only exposure.

The children of Israel experienced this pattern in Egypt. Over generations, they lived among a people whose customs, values, and systems were not their own. Though they remained distinct in origin, they were immersed in a culture that shaped their daily existence. What they saw, they learned. What they learned, they practiced. What they practiced, they carried.

Assimilation does not immediately remove identity. It obscures it. A people who once knew who they were became uncertain about their identity and their belonging. Fragments remain, enough to sense that something has changed, but not enough to restore what was lost. This creates tension. A sense that something is misaligned, without the clarity to identify what it is.

This is why assimilation is subtle. It does not announce itself as replacement. It presents itself as adaptation. The shift is rarely abrupt. It unfolds in stages. What is unfamiliar becomes accepted. What is accepted becomes established. What is established governs until what was original is no longer recognized. Eventually, the original standard is no longer the reference point — something else has taken its place.

This is how identity becomes displaced — through substitution. What was once known begins to fade, not because it has lost its validity, but because it is no longer reinforced. In its absence, something else fills the space. What fills the space begins to define what is lived.

The children of Israel, though removed from Egypt, did not immediately function as a people free from its influence. What was established externally had taken root internally. They were no longer in Egypt, but Egypt remained in them. This reveals the deeper effect of assimilation. It alters what is recognized as normal. Once the standard has shifted, alignment becomes difficult — not because truth is absent, but because it is no longer familiar.

This is where conflict emerges. The call to return confronts conditioning. It challenges what has been accepted. It disrupts what has been normalized. It exposes what has been established. In doing so, it creates resistance. This resistance comes from within. What has been lived becomes a comfort that must be defended. A new standard has been established, and restoration requires an awareness that is not yet present. It requires separation from what has been internalized as normal but does not align with what is true.

Assimilation, therefore, is not simply about adopting what is external. It is about replacing what was original. Until what has been replaced is recognized, what was established will continue to govern what is lived.

A STIFF-NECKED PEOPLE

Stiff-necked is not merely a description of Israel's behavior; it is a diagnosis of their condition. They had become a people resistant to God. Their physical captivity hardened them. What they endured over time produced distrust, resistance, and a hardened will. A people once responsive and obedient had become stubborn and unwilling to be led.

Their struggle with God did not stem from a lack of evidence of His power, but from a perception shaped by years of bondage. They learned to see captivity as familiar and freedom as threatening. What restrained them felt secure. What liberated them felt uncertain. Prolonged oppression afflicts the body and reshapes the will.

Stiff-necked, therefore, is not a simple label. It reveals the tension between divine direction and human resistance. God calls His people forward, yet they hesitate to follow. He leads, yet they resist. Israel became a living example of what transformation looks like after prolonged bondage. Deliverance occurred, but alignment had not yet been restored.

To fully emerge from bondage requires more than physical release. It requires liberation of the body, strengthening of the will, and renewal of the mind. This is not immediate; it is a process, one that unfolds wherever systems have conditioned God's people to remain controlled.

God's call to Israel at Mount Sinai marked the beginning of this transformation. He was not merely forming a nation; He was reshaping a people. He brought them out of Egypt and unto Himself. He was not promising independence; He was establishing relationship. When the children of Israel arrived at Mount Sinai, God instructed Moses to remind them of what they had witnessed:

> *"Ye have seen what I did unto the Egyptians, and how I bare you on eagles' wings, and brought you unto myself. Now therefore, if ye will obey my voice indeed, and keep my covenant, then ye shall be a peculiar treasure unto me above all people… an holy nation."*

> (Exodus 19:4–6)

God revealed Himself through power, deliverance, and provision — making clear who He is and who they were to be in Him — His treasured possession, a kingdom of priests, and a holy nation. The people responded:

> *"And all the people answered together, and said, All that the Lord hath spoken we will do..."*
>
> (Exodus 19:8)

To guide Israel through their transformation, God gave them laws and commandments. Through Moses, He established structure, providing the order necessary to sustain them and realign them with Himself.

> *"Thou shalt have no other gods before me…"*
>
> (Exodus 20:3)

This, the first commandment, was foundational. In adopting the customs of foreign nations, God's people would eventually turn to graven images, giving them the worship that belonged to Him alone. This was not immediate rebellion — it was gradual displacement. Participation led to acceptance. Acceptance led to normalization. Normalization led to substitution. Over time, what was once rejected became established.

This is how Israel turned away from God, not through sudden rejection, but through gradual influence. Pressure shaped their thinking. Fear weakened their resolve. Familiarity replaced conviction, and in that shift, the first commandment was not openly defied — it was quietly displaced. God warned:

> *"Thou shalt not bow down thyself to them, nor serve them: for I the Lord thy God am a jealous God…"*
>
> (Exodus 20:5)

What God forbids in the first commandment extends beyond carved images. It includes anything elevated into a position of authority, reverence, or dependence in place of God. This pattern continues. People are elevated. Systems are trusted. Influence replaces truth. Instead of looking to God, many look to others for answers that can only be found in Him.

The pursuit of gain replaces the pursuit of truth. What is temporary is valued above what is eternal. Yet the instruction remains:

> *"Observe and hear all these words which I command thee, that it may go well with thee, and with thy children after thee forever ..."*
>
> (Deuteronomy 12:28)

When Moses ascended Mount Sinai to receive God's instruction, the people felt his absence. In less than forty days, they turned. They desired a god they could see, and touch, a reflection of what they had learned in captivity. They said:

> *"Up, make us gods, which shall go before us..."*
>
> (Exodus 32:1)

Aaron complied. He collected their gold, formed a calf, and they declared:

> *"These be thy gods, O Israel, which brought thee up out of the land of Egypt."*
>
> (Exodus 32:4)

Consider the weight of this moment.

They replaced the God who delivered them with something they created. They credited their deliverance to what man's hands had formed. This was not ignorance. It was displacement. God's response was immediate:

> *"They have turned aside quickly… they have made them a molten calf, and have worshipped it… I have seen this people, and behold, it is a stiff-necked people."*
>
> (Exodus 32:8–9)

God's anger revealed His grief. He spoke of them as "your people" to Moses, distancing Himself from their actions. Yet Moses interceded. He appealed to God's covenant, reminding Him:

> *"And Moses said…LORD, why doth thy wrath wax hot against **thy people…"***
>
> (Exodus 32:7-11)

God relented. God loves His people. He leads, corrects, and instructs them, not to control them, but to restore them. His commands were not restrictions; they were protection. He warned them not to adopt the customs of the nations they would encounter:

> *"Take heed to thyself that thou be not snared by following them… enquire not after their gods…"*
>
> (Deuteronomy 12:29–31)

To follow their practices would be to adopt their systems, their values, and their gods. It would be to replace what God had established. But God did not leave them without help. He gave them the Law to reveal His standard, guide them, and direct them. Through it they were shown what alignment required. It eventually exposed their inability to sustain it on their own.

This is precisely why, through Christ, God has given us the Holy Spirit. We are guided by what is within, not what is without.

> *"The Comforter will come, which is the Holy Ghost, whom the Father will send in my name, He shall teach you all things, and bring all things to your remembrance, whatsoever I have said unto you."*
>
> (John 14:26)

Dependence on God may feel unfamiliar, but the alternative is far more dangerous. No system, leader, or source of knowledge can replace the guidance of the Holy Spirit. Therefore, we are called to guard what God has given. To resist repeating the same pattern. To refuse both visible idols and invisible ones, whether formed by hand or established in the heart.

Anything that takes the place of God is a betrayal of the relationship He established. That pattern must be broken if we are to love Him with all our heart, all our soul, and all our might.

(See Appendix B — Deuteronomy 32:20: Faith or
Belief)

BONDAGE AS CONDITION, NOT LOCATION

Bondage is often understood as a physical condition — chains, oppression, forced labor, and visible restraint. It is commonly associated with limitation imposed from the outside, where another's authority restricts one's freedom. But bondage, in its most enduring form, is not sustained by what confines the body — it is sustained by what shapes the mind.

A person may be removed from a place of captivity and remain bound. Not because the environment has not changed, but because perception has not. What was once endured externally can be carried internally — reproduced in thought, reinforced through belief, and expressed through behavior.

This is the nature of bondage. It does not require chains to persist. It requires agreement. When a pattern of living is experienced long enough, it begins to establish itself as normal. What was once resisted becomes familiar. What becomes familiar is accepted, and what is accepted begins to define identity. Over time, bondage is no longer recognized as bondage. It is reinterpreted as stability.

This is why departure from bondage can feel like loss. Freedom introduces uncertainty. It removes what was predictable and replaces it with what must be navigated. For one who has adapted to limitation, the absence of constraint can feel disorienting. What is unfamiliar is often perceived as unsafe, even when it is necessary.

Bondage is not only about restriction — it is about conditioning. It teaches dependence, reshapes expectation, and narrows perception. It convinces the individual that what is available is all that exists. Once this belief is established, the need for external control diminishes. The individual begins to maintain the limitation internally. This is where bondage becomes most effective. Not when it is imposed, but when it is sustained.

Throughout history, this pattern has been evident. The children of Israel, though delivered from Egypt, carried with them the imprint of what they had endured. Though removed from the system that confined them, they continued to interpret their reality through the lens of what shaped them. Their environment changed, but their understanding was slower to recover. They remembered what was familiar. They questioned what was new. In moments of discomfort, they desired to return, not because bondage was better, but because it was known.

This reveals the deeper conflict. Bondage does not compete with freedom on the basis of truth — it competes on the basis of familiarity. Familiarity, when left unexamined, can override what is true. This is why transformation requires more than movement. It requires renewal. The mind must be reoriented. Perception must be corrected. Understanding must be restored. Without this, a person may leave bondage physically while remaining bound internally.

True freedom is not simply the absence of restraint — it is the presence of alignment with God. It is the ability to see clearly, to choose rightly, and to walk in what was once resisted.

> *Freedom is not given; it is entered, and it requires participation.*

Bondage, therefore, is not merely something to escape. It is something to be unlearned, because until what has been internalized is confronted, what is believed to have been left behind will continue to live within. What remains within will continue to shape what is lived without.

What was needed was not merely a change of location or circumstance — it was instruction. A standard. A structure that could reorient what bondage had distorted. God's response to this condition was the Law.

CHAPTER 5 — THE LAW: INSTRUCTION TO FULFILLMENT

The law was given by Moses, but grace and truth came by Jesus Christ.

(John 1:17)

Transformation was required. God responded with structure. Bondage revealed a deeper condition — one that could not be corrected by a change of location alone. What was formed internally required more than deliverance; it required direction. God responded by giving His Law.

The Law was not given to restrict them; it was given to sustain them.

Laws are rules established by an authority to maintain order. Without them, society would descend into disorder. While following law is a choice, the consequences of breaking it are not. As a result, we conform to laws, not from conscious obedience, but from conditioned behavior.

When training children to be law-abiding, we often overlook the value of obedience itself. Obedience is not merely behavioral; it is foundational. It establishes alignment. The Laws of God function in the same way. They are given as instruction, establishing order, cultivating accountability, and embedding His standard among His people. They are often misunderstood. Too often, God's Law is viewed through the lens of correction alone. It is associated with penance, fear, and restriction. To reduce it to punishment is to overlook its purpose, its benefit, and its promise.

God's Law is instruction designed to shape behavior in alignment with His intent. Just as we train our children to function within societal order, so too must we learn to respond to God's instruction. Yet within this, a deeper tension exists.

Even today, the Law remains widely misunderstood — its relationship to God's love obscured. How do these passages agree?

> *"Think not that I am come to destroy the law, or the prophets: I am not come to destroy, but to fulfil."*
>
> (Matthew 5:17)

> *"For verily I say unto you, **Till heaven and earth pass,** one jot or one tittle shall in no wise pass from the law, till all be fulfilled."*
>
> (Matthew 5:18)

> ***"For as many as are of the works of the law** are under the cursed for it is written, Cursed is every one that continueth not in all things which are written in the book of the law to do them."*
>
> (Galatians 3:10)

Together, these passages reveal movement — not contradiction, but progression toward fulfillment. Verse seventeen affirms permanence in the Law, while verse eighteen introduces a condition of fulfillment, "till heaven and earth pass" indicates movement toward completion.

Galatians 3:10 could lead one to believe everyone who does not follow the Law perfectly is universally condemned. However, "For as many as are of the works of the law" clarifies this pertains to anyone relying on works of the Law rather than faith.

Read together, they do not contradict — they progress. The Law established the standard. Fulfillment completed what the standard pointed toward.

This is not contradiction — it is context.

The Law reveals God's standard, but it also exposes man's inability to sustain it. It was never meant to stand alone. It points beyond itself.

> *"Wherefore the law was our schoolmaster to bring*
> *us unto Christ that we might be justified by faith"*
> (Galatians 3:24)

The Law was the guide — not the destination. It illuminated the path, but it could not complete the journey. As declared at the outset — the Law came through Moses, but grace and truth came through Christ.

TWO LAWS

The Old Covenant reveals two expressions of law given to the children of Israel: that which was temporal and that which is unchanging.

The temporal, or Hebraic Law, often referred to as the Law of Moses, was conditional and temporary. It included sacrifices, rituals, and restrictions designed to address transgression and regulate behavior. These laws functioned as a bridge, guiding God's people until fulfillment would come.

The unchanging Law consists of divine principles that reflect the nature of God Himself. These laws establish moral order and are not subject to change. As declared among the covenant curses at Mount Ebal:

> *Cursed be the man that maketh any graven or molten image... Cursed be he that setteth light by his father or his mother... Cursed be he that removeth his neighbour's landmark...*
>
> (Deuteronomy 27:15–26)
> *(See Appendix A for how misinterpretation of these laws has produced substitution.)*

These laws revealed not only the consequence of disobedience but the standard by which God's people were to be known. Jesus affirmed this:

> *"Whosoever therefore shall break one of these least commandments, and shall teach men so, he shall be called the least in the kingdom of heaven: but whosoever shall do and teach them, the same shall be called great in the kingdom of heaven."*
>
> (Matthew 5:19)

God does not change; those who align with Him are strengthened and sustained. Yet even those who had received what the Law pointed toward were not immune to returning to what it replaced. The Galatians received grace, yet returned to works, relying on what was familiar rather than what was revealed.

"For sin shall not have dominion over you: for ye are not under the law, but under grace."

(Romans 6:14)

"O foolish Galatians... Received ye the Spirit by the works of the law, or by the hearing of faith having begun in the Spirit, are ye now made perfect by the flesh?"

(Galatians 3:1–3)

The Galatians were not being drawn back to the unchanging moral Law — they were retreating to the temporal works-based system that Christ had already fulfilled. They were returning to the bridge after reaching the other side. They were not lacking truth — they were at a crossroads of transformation. Their renewal in the Spirit was not familiar. Familiarity with bondage had given them a false sense of stability. What once constrained them now felt secure. To return to it was not an uncomfortable stretch, but a retreat into an imitation of peace.

This was the same pull that drew Israel back toward Egypt in the wilderness — not because Egypt was better, but because it was known. What a people endure long enough does not remain external. It becomes internal. It is carried forward through generations, shaping response, perception, and instinct long after the original condition has passed. The Galatians were not simply reverting to works — they were responding to something embedded far deeper than conscious choice.

But for the Gentiles among them, the pull was no less real. This is the condition of the natural man. He does not distrust God out of rebellion alone — he distrusts what he cannot see, cannot measure, and cannot control. What requires faith feels unstable. What requires works feels safe. And so he returns — not to truth, but to the familiar. Not to freedom, but to the form of it. This is not only the condition of the Galatians. It is the condition of every person who has not yet allowed the Spirit to do what the flesh never could — submit wholly to God.

FULFILLMENT OF THE LAW

The Law is based on works. Salvation is by grace through faith.

Christ is the fulfillment of what the Law pointed toward.

> *"For Christ is the end of the law for righteousness to every one that believeth."*
>
> (Romans 10:4)

The Law functioned as a bridge — it carried God's people toward what was coming. When Christ came, He fulfilled what the Law revealed. Christ did not redeem us from the Law. He redeemed us from its curse. The curse was not the Law itself — it was the consequence of failing to keep it completely. Moses declared it plainly:

> *"Cursed is every one that continueth not in all things which are written in the book of the law to do them."*
>
> (Deuteronomy 27:26)

Every person stood under that curse. Not because the Law was unjust, but because no person could sustain what it required. The Law was not the problem. The inability to fulfill it was. Paul described this conflict plainly:

> *"For I delight in the law of God after the inward man: For I see another law in my members, warring against the law of my mind, and bringing*

*me into captivity to the law of sin which is in my
members."*

(Romans 7:22–23)

The inward man desired alignment. The flesh could not produce it. This is what Christ addressed. He did not set the Law aside — he bore its full weight on behalf of those who could not.

> *"Christ hath redeemed us from the curse of the law..."*

(Galatians 3:13)

The Law reveals what is required. Grace provides what we cannot. Salvation is not earned — it is received. Not through effort, but through faith.

> *"For by grace are ye saved through faith; and that not of yourselves: it is the gift of God: not of works, lest any man should boast."*

(Ephesians 2:8–9)

Christ bore that weight. Paul writes:

> *"Who gave himself for our sins, that he might deliver us..."*

(Galatians 1:4)

Christ came to rescue us from a condition shaped by influence, sustained by patterns, and internalized through experience. He delivered us from what governed us. Yet the pull toward what is familiar remains.

> *"I marvel that ye are so soon removed from Him that called you into the grace of Christ unto another gospel."*

(Galatians 1:6)

The Galatians returned to what was familiar because familiarity, even when it leads to bondage, feels like stability.

Christ is our atonement.
He is our justification.
He is our hope.

His salvation comes by grace through faith. Through Him, what the Law revealed is fulfilled.

CHAPTER 6 — THE ILLUSION OF FREEDOM

And ye shall know the truth, and the truth shall make you free.

(John 8:32)

Freedom is often defined by the absence of visible restraint. It is measured by the ability to choose, to move, to act without interference. It is associated with independence, self-direction, self-expression, and autonomy.

What is commonly understood as freedom, however, is not always what it appears to be, because the absence of restriction does not guarantee the presence of truth.

A person may be free to choose yet bound in what they choose from. This is the illusion.

Freedom is not only about options — it is about alignment. When the standard by which choices are made has been altered, freedom becomes limited without appearing so. The individual believes they are operating independently, yet their decisions are shaped by influences they no longer recognize.

What is perceived as freedom is often guided by unseen constraints. Preferences are formed. Desires are shaped. Perspectives are framed — all within boundaries that are rarely questioned. This is how freedom becomes simulated — not through force, but through influence. The individual is not prevented from choosing; they are conditioned in how they choose.

Over time, this conditioning becomes invisible. What has been learned feels natural. What has been repeated feels right. What feels right is rarely examined. What is familiar is trusted, even when it is misaligned. This is where the illusion is sustained.

This is why true freedom cannot be defined by movement alone. A person may move freely yet think within limits. Speak freely yet perceive inaccurately. Act independently yet remain internally governed by what has never been questioned.

This is not freedom. It is managed autonomy.

The boundaries remain, but they have been internalized. Because they are internal, they are rarely resisted. This reveals something essential: freedom is not proven by the ability to act. It is revealed by the ability to discern — to see clearly. To distinguish between what is true and what has been inherited. Without this, freedom becomes performance — an expression of choice within a system that has already defined the options.

This is why truth must precede freedom. Without truth, freedom has no reference point. It becomes directionless, guided not by what is right, but by what is available. What is available is not always what is aligned.

The illusion of freedom, therefore, is not the absence of control — it is the presence of control that is no longer recognized. It is the belief that one is free while remaining shaped by what has never been questioned.

WHAT ALIGNMENT LOOKS LIKE PRACTICALLY

Alignment is revealed in patterns. It is established by how you respond. To walk with God is to bring your life into agreement with Him — consistently, intentionally, and without compromise. This begins with submission. It is not forced; it is chosen.

To align is to yield your will where it conflicts with His. It is to move from preference to obedience. From self-direction to God-direction.

Alignment is revealed in response. When correction comes, do you resist, or do you adjust? When conviction comes, do you ignore it, or do you act? When instruction is given, do you delay, or do you follow?

Alignment is consistency. It is the refusal to remain in failure; it is returning, realigning, and pressing forward.

Alignment is expressed in relationships. To love God is to obey Him. To love others is to show who He is. You must live in the truth. You must demonstrate faith.

Alignment must be maintained. Just as a vehicle requires periodic correction to remain properly aligned, so does a life. Small deviations left unaddressed lead to larger consequences over time. It is subtle; it happens gradually — through neglect, distraction, and compromise. What was once clear becomes blurred. What was once firm becomes flexible.

Alignment requires awareness. You must examine your life. Are your decisions consistent with what you believe? Does your conduct reflect what you claim? Are you moving in the direction God has established — or in one you have chosen?

Alignment produces stability. When you are aligned, your direction is steady; your movement is purposeful. Your life reflects order because there is agreement. Where there is agreement, there is unity.

Alignment is not achieved once. It is maintained — daily, deliberately, continuously.

True freedom is not found in the expansion of options. It is found in alignment with what is true, because only what is true can liberate what has been bound.

Israel would demonstrate this pattern — choosing not from ignorance, but from preference. That choice and its consequences is where we turn next.

CHAPTER 7 — THE PATTERN OF SUBSTITUTION

I call heaven and earth to record this day against you, that I have set before you life and death... therefore choose life...

(Deuteronomy 30:19)

THE POLITICAL SHIFT

When Israel asked for a king, they were not merely changing leadership; they were changing systems. They were moving from dependence on God to dependence on man.

God warned them through Samuel. He told them what would follow: control, taxation, oppression, and burden. Yet they insisted on a king.

This was the turning point. They did not lack guidance. They rejected it. There comes a moment when what is true is revealed, yet what is familiar is still chosen. Awareness does not eliminate choice. It exposes it.

A PATTERN OF DEPENDENCE

Israel knew God as their source. He delivered them, sustained them, and went before them in battle. Yet their dependence began to shift. The presence of mediators created a subtle distance. From that point forward, what was once intimate became managed. What was once relational began to resemble structure.

This shift did not begin with rejection; it began with reliance. Reliance on what was seen, reliance on what was familiar, and reliance on man. It was into this condition that Samuel was raised — a man appointed to speak where God's people had grown accustomed to hearing through others. Yet God never withdrew. Even as dependence shifted toward the visible, He continued to speak — adapting how He reached His people without changing who He is. Though the way His people approach Him remained constant, the way He engaged them unfolded in stages.

There were times when God spoke directly, as with Adam and Abraham, establishing instruction and calling them to lead. There were times when He spoke through conduits, as with Moses, Joshua, and Samuel — men appointed to deliver His word to the people. There is now revelation through the Holy Spirit, accessed through Jesus Christ.

Each transition followed moments of failure, resistance, or misalignment, revealing that substitution was often God's response to what His people could no longer sustain. Yet the transition from mediation through men to revelation through Christ carries the greatest significance, for it defines the path to restoration.

Samuel was born into faithfulness. His father, Elkanah, was a man who honored God's appointed order, and his mother, Hannah, trusted in the power of God. Samuel himself was given as a result of prayer and returned to God as an offering.

Raised under Eli, he grew in obedience and found favor with both God and Israel. As Eli's strength declined, God began to speak directly to Samuel and establish him as a prophet.

> *"And Samuel grew, and the LORD was with him,*
> *and did let none of his words fall to the ground.*
> *And all Israel... knew that Samuel was established*
> *to be a prophet of the LORD."*
>
> (1 Samuel 3:19–20)

Samuel became a vessel — one through whom God spoke to His people.

THE REQUEST FOR A KING

When Samuel's sons failed to uphold righteousness, the elders of Israel faced uncertainty. Yet rather than seeking God, they sought structure through man.

> *"Then all the elders of Israel gathered themselves*
> *together, and came to Samuel unto Ramah, And*
> *said unto him, Behold, thou art old, and thy sons*
> *walk not in thy ways: now make us a king to judge*
> *us like all the nations."*
>
> (1 Samuel 8:4-5)

This request was not merely political; it was spiritual. They desired to be like other nations, but what the nations possessed was not what made Israel distinct. Men governed other nations. God governed Israel. In asking for a king, they were not solving a problem; they were replacing their source.

> *"And the LORD said unto Samuel,* Hearken unto
> the voice of the people in all that they say unto

thee: *they have not rejected thee, but they have
rejected me, that I should not reign over them."*

(1 Samuel 8:7)

This was the choice, not between leadership structures, but
between God and man. God did not conceal the consequences.
Through Samuel, He revealed what life under a human king
would require.

Their sons would be taken; their daughters would serve;
their land would be claimed; their labor would be used, and they
would become subject to what they had chosen. Yet even with full
knowledge, they refused correction.

*"Nevertheless the people refused to obey the voice
of Samuel; and they said, Nay; but we will have a
king over us; ... That we also may be like all the
nations..."*

(1 Samuel 8:19–20)

This is the nature of false choice. It is not made in ignorance, but
in preference.

THE TURNING POINT

This was not simply disobedience — it was substitution. They
replaced God with man. They chose to be like other nations rather
than remain set apart. What was once unthinkable became
acceptable. What was acceptable became normal. From that
moment forward, turning away from God would not be the
exception, but the pattern.

God had chosen His people to be distinct above all nations.
Yet Israel chose imitation over distinction. God went before them
and fought their battles, yet they preferred a man to fight for them.
God rescued them in their need, yet they looked to man for help.

God guided them when they were lost, yet they chose man for direction.

At every turn, God was present. At every turn they looked elsewhere.

God chose Israel, and Israel rejected God.

THE NORMALIZATION OF SUBSTITUTION

God granted their request. Over time, submission to human authority became a new normal for the children of Israel, a pattern that would extend far beyond their land and into the generations that followed.

As they were scattered and assimilated among other nations, this dependence deepened. Their hearts and minds were reconditioned. Man-made systems of authority became the standard, eventually accepted as unavoidable. But beneath this normalized submission, the original standard had not been removed. It is deception to believe that God's people must align themselves with human systems to preserve their identity. Systems are designed to maintain order, but they also sustain a level of dependence that can replace reliance on God.

What begins as structure can become substitution. What begins as governance can become control. Control, when normalized, is rarely questioned. Yet God's people always have a choice, regardless of time, season, or system.

Israel's betrayal was not a single moment. It was a pattern — documented, progressive, and warned against before it ever occurred. The record in 2 Kings traces what that turning produced.

They feared false gods:

> *"The children of Israel had sinned against the LORD their God... and had feared other gods."*
>
> (2 Kings 17:7)

They followed pagan practices:

> *"And walked in the statutes of the heathen, whom the LORD cast out before the children of Israel."*
>
> (2 Kings 17:8)

God instructed them plainly at Sinai. Two things were required:

> *Obey my voice.*
> *Guard my covenant.*

They did neither:

> *"And they left all the commandments of the LORD their God, and made them molten images, even two calves... and served Baal."*
>
> (2 Kings 17:16)

They sacrificed their children:

> *"And they caused their sons and their daughters to pass through the fire."*
>
> (2 Kings 17:17)

They practiced witchcraft:

> *"...and used divination and enchantments, and sold themselves to do evil in the sight of the LORD."*
>
> (2 Kings 17:17 cont.)

The consequence was removal:

> *"Therefore the LORD was very angry with Israel and removed them out of his sight: there was none left but the tribe of Judah only."*
>
> (2 Kings 17:18)

Judah followed the same path:

> *"Also Judah kept not the commandments of the LORD their God but walked in the statutes of Israel which they made."*
>
> (2 Kings 17:19)

> *"And the LORD rejected all the seed of Israel and afflicted them... until he had cast them out of his sight."*
>
> (2 Kings 17:20)

None of this was without warning. God revealed what would follow long before it occurred. That one decision — to choose a king over God — set this pattern in motion, shaping Israel's identity, its scattering, and its condition to this present day.

(See Appendix B — Deuteronomy 32:20: Faith or Belief)

The normalization of human authority did not remain contained to Israel alone. It spread — across generations, across borders, and across systems of governance that would shape the world long after Israel's kingdom had fallen.

As God's people were scattered among the nations, they entered systems already established. They did not build these structures — they inherited them. In inheriting them, they adapted to them. What was once foreign became familiar. What became familiar became accepted. What was accepted became the framework through which identity, governance, and even faith were understood.

SYSTEMS OF MEN

From that point forward, what was once direct became mediated. What was once revealed became instructed. What was once spiritual became institutional.

These inherited systems required allegiance. They shaped behavior; they influenced thought; they established boundaries. In doing so, they subtly replaced reliance on God with reliance on structure. Systems do not always remove truth. More often, they reinterpret it, restructure it, and present it in a form that can be sustained without alignment.

Scripture instructs believers to resolve matters within the body, rather than placing them before secular systems. This reflects a higher order — one governed by alignment, not external authority.

> *"Dare any of you, having a matter against another, go to law before the unjust, and not before the saints?"*
>
> (1 Corinthians 6:1)
>
> *(See Appendix A for how misinterpretation has produced substitution.)*

What something is called matters. Names carry meaning. Meaning shapes understanding. Understanding directs alignment. From the beginning, what God established was defined with purpose.

> *"And God said, Let there be lights in the firmament of the heaven to divide the day from the night; and let them be for signs, and for seasons, and for days, and years."*
>
> (Genesis 1:14)

Time was not defined by human systems but by divine function and order. Over time, systems developed that replaced what was originally established.

Days were named. Months were named. Systems were introduced. What was once observed through alignment became observed through structure.

> *(See Appendix C for a full study of calendar systems and the naming of days.)*

Scripture reveals that the manipulation of time is not incidental — it is intentional.

> *"And he shall speak great words against the Most High... and think to change times and laws..."*
>
> (Daniel 7:25)

Time, in Scripture, is not merely a measurement; it is structure. It is order. It is alignment. When time is altered, understanding is altered, and when understanding is altered, alignment is disrupted. God established the commandment plainly:

> *"Remember the Sabbath day, to keep it holy."*
>
> (Exodus 20:8)

This command is unique. It is both a law and a specific point in time. If the time is misunderstood, the command is misapplied. If the command is misapplied, what was intended to align becomes something that does not. Not enough to appear false, but enough to move it out of alignment.

The political pattern had been established. The systems of men had taken root. What remained was the extension of that pattern into what was meant to be sacred — and the substitution that followed was no less deliberate.

CHAPTER 8 — THE ECCLESIASTICAL SHIFT

Howbeit in vain do they worship me, teaching for doctrines the commandments of men.

(Mark 7:7)

The pattern of substitution did not remain political. It extended into what was meant to be spiritual. Systems were built, structures were formed, and authority was assigned. What was once revealed became regulated, and what was once received became taught as doctrine alone. The Spirit was no longer the primary guide; interpretation was. Over time, dependence shifted again. From God to systems that claimed to represent Him.

Not all error comes from rejection. Some of it comes from misinterpretation. What is written can be read and still not be understood.

Scripture, when taken without context, can be used to justify what was never intended. What was given as instruction can be reshaped into permission. This is how substitution occurs. Not by removing truth, but by redefining it.

A single passage, isolated from its context, can appear to contradict what was clearly established. When interpretation replaces alignment, confusion follows.

God is consistent. What He establishes does not contradict itself. When something opposes what has already been spoken, it is not truth that has shifted; it is understanding that has been misapplied.

This is why discernment is required, not to rely on intellect, but to be led by the Spirit. Not everything that is read is rightly divided. Not everything that is taught is aligned.

THE ILLUSION OF REPRESENTATION

These systems do not represent the fullness of what God established. They maintain order, they organize belief, but they do not replace the Spirit. God's children are not required to submit fully to any human system in order to live in truth. No government, no institution, no structure can stand in the place of God. Yet for many, these systems have done precisely that — quietly, consistently, and without recognition.

God's children have always had a choice, not bound by time, and not limited by system. They have a choice to choose Him or to replace Him. Israel chose a king. That choice became a pattern. A pattern of turning to man instead of God. Jesus is the way. Not a system built in His name. Not a structure claiming His authority. The way itself. There will always be choices. But the instruction is clear — do not turn to the left or to the right. Walk straight.

"Only be thou strong and very courageous, that thou mayest observe to do according to all the law, which Moses my servant commanded thee: turn not from it to the right hand or to the left, that thou mayest prosper whithersoever thou goest."

(Joshua 1:7)

There will always be those who claim Christ as the foundation of what they have built. That claim alone is not enough. What matters is whether the path leads to Him or away from Him.

We are not called to follow what bears His name. We are called to follow Him.

The systems had been identified. The pattern had been named. What remained was the answer — and the answer was not another system. It was a person.

RESTORATION THROUGH JESUS CHRIST

Jesus entered into a world already structured by political, religious, and social systems. He did not conform to them. He challenged them. He stood in the midst of authority and declared:

> *"Jesus said unto him, I am the way, the truth, and the life: no man cometh unto the Father, but by me."*

(John 14:6)

He did not present an alternative system; He presented Himself. He did not present one option among many; He revealed the only way. He did not bring answers; He is the answer. Even now, He remains unchanged, declaring what has always been true.

The solution has never been found in systems. It is found in the Father.

THE RETURN

Israel was already in covenant with God. That covenant had not been broken by God; it had been neglected by His people. God chose Israel. Yet Israel chose man. The way back is not through systems, but through surrender. Through obedience. Through choosing Him again. To choose Him is to restore what was broken.

This is what salvation is. Not the adoption of another system, but the return to the Father. Not dependence on structure, but restoration of relationship. Not instruction alone, but transformation through the Spirit. As declared at the outset — life and death remain set before you.

This choice has never been removed. It remains, across time, across systems, across generations. To choose God is to return to alignment. To choose otherwise is to repeat the pattern.

History does not correct itself; it must be confronted. Israel experienced God's faithfulness repeatedly yet continued to turn away when comfort returned. Their disobedience was not always rooted in ignorance, but in forgetfulness of who God was and who they were in relation to Him.

Even today, many are aware of fragments of their history, yet substitute it with what is visible, measurable, and immediate. To return to God requires more than acknowledgment; it requires reconciliation. Reconciliation of what has been learned with what is true. Scripture and ancient record both confirm this was not unforeseen:

> *"I will hide my face from them, and I will deliver them into the hand of the other nations for captivity ... and I will remove them from the midst of the land, and I will scatter them amongst the other nations. And they will forget all my Torah and all my commandments..."*
>
> (Jubilees 1:14–15 Eth Cepher)

Yet God remains longsuffering. Return begins with recognition. It continues with repentance. Not only for personal actions, but for patterns that have been inherited.

"I know their contrariness and their thoughts and their stiff-kneckedness, and they will not be obedient till they confess their own sin and the sin of their fathers."

(Jubilees 1:23 Eth Cepher)

Though the effects of disobedience have been carried across generations, responsibility remains individual. We must choose. God has not withdrawn Himself. Even in dispersion, even in distance, even in misalignment. He remains.

"And they will return to me… and I will gather them…"

(Jubilees 1:16 Eth Cepher)

He restores. He re-establishes. He renews.

"And I will be their God, and they shall be my people…"

(Jubilees 1:18 Eth Cepher)

Only through the Holy Spirit — restoring what was severed, revealing what was replaced — could the way back be found.

The path back has never changed. It begins with a choice.

CHAPTER 9 — SEPARATION AND REVELATION

My sheep hear my voice, and I know them, and they
follow me.

(John 10:27)

Peter is referred to throughout Scripture as Simon, Peter, Simon Peter, and Simon who is called Peter. Yet before the account in Matthew chapter 16, Jesus does not address him by these names directly.

In this moment, however, Jesus calls him with intention:

"... Blessed art thou, Simon Barjona: for flesh and
blood hath not revealed it unto thee, but my Father
which is in heaven."

(Matthew 16:17)

The name Simon is associated with hearing — one who listens with attention and intent. This is who he was. This moment would reveal who he was becoming.

THE QUESTION

When Jesus came into the coasts of Caesarea Philippi, He asked His disciples a defining question:

> *"… Whom do men say that I the Son of man am?"*
> (Matthew 16:13)

They answered:

> *"… Some say that thou art John the Baptist: some, Elias; and others, Jeremias, or one of the prophets."*
> (Matthew 16:14)

These answers were formed through observation. But Jesus pressed further:

> *"He said unto them, But whom say ye that I am?"*
> (Matthew 16:15)

THE FATHER SPEAKS

When Jesus asked, "Whom say ye that I am?" He was not asking for information — He was revealing a distinction. Peter responded:

> *"… Thou art the Christ, the Son of the living God."*
> (Matthew 16:16)

Jesus answered him:

> *"… Blessed art thou, Simon Barjon: for flesh and blood hath not revealed it unto thee, but my Father which is in heaven."*
> (Matthew 16:17)

This was not taught. It was revealed. Peter did not arrive at this understanding through study, nor through instruction — but through direct reception from the Father. This is the foundation. One that cannot be constructed, only received.

THE ROCK: REVELATION AS FOUNDATION

Jesus then said:

> *"...thou art Peter, and upon this rock I will build my church..."*
>
> (Matthew 16:18)

The Rock is not the man. It is the revelation.

Peter's transformation in that moment was not external. It was internal. He no longer heard with attention alone; he received with alignment.

God's people were lost. They were disconnected from Him. The intimacy of that connection severed when they chose a man to represent them in God's place. Peter, receiving directly from the Father, was the re-establishment of that relationship.

God provided the Law as a bridge — temporary, sufficient for its purpose, pointing toward what was to be permanent. Jesus was the solution. He was sent to reestablish a more permanent connection.

---
*He came to restore what had been severed
between God and His people. He died to extend
that restoration to the world.*

Not doctrine. Not institution. Not a man. Revelation.

*(See Appendix B — Lexical Study: Simon, Peter,
Rock, and Cephas)*

THE INDWELLING

What occurred in Peter is the model. To receive directly from God, not through reasoning, not through assumption, but through revelation.

> *"But the natural man receiveth not the things of the Spirit of God: for they are foolishness unto him: neither can he know them, because they are spiritually discerned."*
>
> (1 Corinthians 2:14)

Man judges from below. God declares from above.

> *"For the wisdom of this world is foolishness with God. For it is written, He taketh the wise in their own craftiness."*
>
> *(1 Corinthians 3:19)*

What is spiritual must be spiritually discerned. Peter had just received from the Father. In doing so, he demonstrated what it means to move beyond natural perception into spiritual understanding.

From this point forward, Jesus began preparing His disciples for what would come next. While He was with them, they looked to Him for instruction, for direction, and for understanding. But this was not the final structure. What was established through His presence would now be sustained through the Spirit:

> *"... It is expedient for you that I go away: for if I go not away, the Comforter will not come unto you; but if I depart, I will send him unto you. I have*

*yet many things to say unto you, but ye cannot hear
them now."*

(John 16:7-12)

*"Howbeit when he, the Spirit of truth, is come, he
will guide you into all truth: for he shall not speak
of himself; but whatsoever he shall hear,* that *shall
he speak: and he will shew you things to come."*

(John 16:13)

The same truth that had been revealed externally would now be
revealed internally. Even after His resurrection, this pattern
remained:

*"But the anointing which ye have received of him
abideth in you, and ye need not that any man teach
you: but as the same anointing teacheth you of all
things..."*

(1 John 2:27)

The source did not change — only the method of access did. This
is the restoration. The relationship between God and His people is
not dependent on proximity — but on alignment. God's children
can now receive directly from Him through the indwelling of the
Holy Spirit. The foundation has not changed. The access has been
restored.

---

*They were once disconnected and misaligned.
Now reconnected, returning to alignment.*

REVELATION AND REJECTION

This moment of revelation was not new in design but it was new
in their experience. They had been governed by kings, priests,

prophets, and systems for generations. Direct reception from the Father was not their current reality — it was their original design that had been buried under centuries of substitution until it was no longer recognized as possible. This was now being restored.

God Himself led Israel directly. His voice was their direction and His presence was their covering. Yet they exchanged direct divine leadership for human authority. They chose what was visible over what required faith.

What Peter had just received — direct revelation from the Father — was the very thing Israel exchanged for a king. What was being restored in Peter in Caesarea Philippi was what had been surrendered at Ramah.

THE QUESTION REMAINS

Revelation establishes what is true, but faith determines whether it is lived. Access has been restored, but access alone is not enough. What is revealed must be received; what is received must be formed, and what is formed must be lived. The question has not changed:

"Whom say ye that I am?"

(Matthew 16:15)

Whom do you say that He is?

CHAPTER 10 — THE INSTABILITY OF PARTIAL FAITH

O ye of little faith, why didst thou doubt?

(Matthew 14:31)

The teachings of Jesus were not abstract ideals. They were not directed to those who opposed Him, but to those who would follow Him — the lost sheep of Israel, called back to alignment.

THE MEASURE OF FAITH

During Jesus' ministry on earth, the disciples operated within the limitations of their understanding, interpreting what they experienced through natural perception.

They witnessed what Jesus could do, and they believed in Him. Yet their belief had not yet matured into alignment.

They would have to be transformed by the renewing of their minds. Only then would they begin to believe on Him — moving from belief to belief, from natural understanding to spiritual alignment. With their vision renewed, they would transition from one system of understanding to another, gradually ascending in awareness as their perception aligned with truth.

> *"For therein is the righteousness of God revealed from belief to belief: as it is written, The just shall live by belief."*
>
> (Romans 1:17, Eth Cepher)

Faith is revealed by response, not determined by exposure. To believe begins with acceptance. It acknowledges that something is true. Belief develops into conviction. It becomes a principle — something held, not merely heard.

Faith is the expression of that conviction. It is belief that is lived and demonstrated through trust, alignment, and action. Faith is born out of belief. Where belief is absent, faith cannot exist.

Precision matters in language. Words that appear similar often carry distinct meanings — and those distinctions, when examined, reveal something essential.

What we believe directs our thought process and can develop into a belief. Our belief determines our course and conduct, producing guiding principles. Faith is the demonstration (inward or outward) of what we initially believed and have developed into a belief.

> *"He that has ears to hear, let him hear."*
>
> (Matthew 11:15)

In the Eth Cepher, the word belief is often used in place of the word faith, compared to the King James Bible. In the King James Version, the word faith appears frequently, while in the Eth Cepher it appears less often, with belief used more extensively. The words faith and belief have been used interchangeably based on their similarities; however, their differences may carry significance in their usage.

The Greek language preserves a distinction that English translations have often obscured. The words believe, belief, and faith are not interchangeable — they represent progressive levels of conscious alignment, each building upon the other. Three words form the foundation of this study:

> **Believe** — pisteuō (4100): to think to be true, to be persuaded of, to place confidence in.
> **Faith** — pistis (4102): conviction of truth; belief accompanied by trust and confidence.
> **Root** — peitho (3982): to persuade, to induce belief, to produce inward certainty.

Both pisteuō and pistis — believe and faith — originate from the root peitho — to persuade. Yet persuasion alone does not produce trust. A person may be persuaded that something is true without ever placing confidence in it. This is the distinction the Greek preserves.

To believe — pisteuō — is the entry point. It is the acceptance of a declaration as true. A person can hear that Jesus is Lord and accept it as true based on that declaration alone. No personal experience is required. No action necessarily follows. Belief has been introduced but not yet established.

Faith — pistis — is not the same starting point. It is conviction. It is belief that has been tested, established, and accompanied by trust. Where pisteuō accepts, pistis acts. Where pisteuō hears, pistis responds. The difference between them is not one of kind but of depth — one is the seed, the other is the fruit.

Between them is the development. What is believed must be examined, reinforced, and lived before it matures into the conviction that pistis describes. This progression is not accidental — it is the pattern God has always used with His people.

"So then belief comes by hearing, and hearing by the Word of God."

(Romaiym 10:17, Eth Cepher)

Hearing produces believing. Believing, when consistently reinforced and lived, develops into belief. Belief, when established as conviction, produces faith. Each stage is necessary. None can be skipped. Each one represents a higher level of conscious alignment with truth.

(See Appendix B — Greek Word Study and Hebrew Understanding for the complete word study)

HEBREW UNDERSTANDING

Where the Greek preserves distinction through precision, the Hebrew adds dimension through depth. The Hebrew language does not merely define these words — it gives them life. What the Greek identifies as stages of progression, the Hebrew expresses as levels of devotion. Three expressions form the foundation of this study:

> **Believe** — leh-ah-meen: to accept or deem something true, to acknowledge without necessarily requiring evidence or proof.
> **Belief** — emunah: a deeper conviction or trust in a certain concept, idea, or principle. It involves personal attachment, devotion, and consecration.
> **Faith** — emunah: steadfast and unwavering trust, confidence, and loyalty — particularly in matters of spiritual significance

To believe → to form a belief → to walk in faith

The Hebrew reveals something the Greek does not surface as directly — believe and belief are distinct in expression, but belief and faith share the same word. Emunah carries both meanings. This is not an oversight. It is intentional.

In Hebrew understanding, belief and faith are not two separate destinations — they are two expressions of the same devotion at different levels of maturity. What begins as conviction deepens into unwavering loyalty. What is established as a principle becomes a way of life. The progression is not merely intellectual — it is relational. It reflects the deepening of a relationship with God.

This is why the Hebrew definition adds what the Greek does not yet name — devotion. To believe in the Hebrew sense is to accept. To hold belief is to be devoted. To walk in faith is to be consecrated — set apart in loyalty and trust.

Consider what this reveals about Israel in Deuteronomy 32:20. God did not look among His people for active trust in a people who had abandoned their devotion entirely. He identified the absence of something more foundational:

> *"...they are a very froward generation, children in whom is no belief."*
> (Devariym 32:20, Eth Cepher)

Where devotion collapses, conviction cannot stand. Where conviction cannot stand, faith has nothing left to rest upon. The Hebrew understanding makes this plain — the progression must be honored. You cannot walk in faith without belief. You cannot hold belief without first believing.

To believe is inward acceptance. Belief is established devotion. Faith is security and action rooted in that devotion.

They are not identical. They are progressive. Each represents a deeper level of conscious alignment with God — moving from acceptance, to conviction, to consecration.

*"But without belief it is impossible to please him:
for he that comes to God must believe that he is
and he is a rewarder of them that diligently seek
him."*

(Ivriym 11:6, Eth Cepher)

One must first believe in order to have belief. One must have belief in order to walk in faith. This is the pattern — in the Greek, in the Hebrew, and throughout Scripture.
(See Appendix B — Hebrews 11: Belief in Action)

BELIEVE/BELIEF/FAITH AND HOPE

Hope is anticipation with expectation and confidence. It is intangible yet inherently present — the forward pull of what has been promised but not yet seen. Hope serves as the power source that fuels belief and faith, leading toward eternal significance.

Without faith it is impossible to please Him.
Without belief it is impossible to know Him.
Without hope it is impossible to endure

Hope extends beyond what is immediate. It is not a dream — it is confident expectation rooted in what God has spoken. Where belief accepts what is true and faith demonstrates what is believed, hope anchors both to what is coming.

*"For we are saved by hope: but hope that is seen
is not hope: for what a man seeth, why doth he yet
hope for? But if we hope for that we see not, then
do we with patience wait for it."*

(Romans 8:24–25)

Hope does not replace belief or faith. It completes the progression.

To believe is to accept what is true. To hold a belief is to be established in what is true. To walk in faith is to demonstrate what is true. To hope is to remain anchored to what is coming — because what God has promised has not yet been fully seen.

(See Appendix B — Hebrews 11: Belief in Action)

BELIEF AS A CATALYST

Placebo treatments — substances with no active medical effect — have been shown to produce measurable improvement in patients who *believe* they are receiving treatment. This does not prove the substance had power, but it demonstrates the influence of belief. Belief produces response. To believe something is the catalyst to change.

Belief is not static. What begins as acceptance must develop into conviction — and that development is not automatic. It requires something more than hearing. Scripture reveals this tension in one of the most honest exchanges recorded between a man and his Savior about his son who had a dumb spirit:

> *"Jesus said unto him, If thou canst believe, all things are possible to him that believeth."*
>
> (Mark 9:23)

The father already accepted that Jesus was capable. His persistence demonstrated that — he first brought his son to the disciples, and when they could not cast the spirit out, he came to Jesus himself. His believing was intact. But believing alone was not enough for what the moment required. He needed belief — established conviction — and he knew he did not yet have it. His response revealed both his honesty and his understanding:

> *"...the father of the child cried out, and said with*
> *tears, Lord, I believe; help thou mine unbelief."*
> *(Mark 9:24)*

This was not a contradiction. It was a declaration of where he was in the progression. He was not without believing. He was without the conviction that believing must become. Rather than pretending otherwise, he brought his limitation directly to Jesus. This is the pattern. Believing is the entry point. But it must develop. Where it has not yet developed, the answer is not pretense — it is surrender.

To witness truth is different from believing it. To follow Christ is different from total confidence in Him. The disciples walked with Jesus. They saw what others could not see. They heard what others could not hear. Yet their faith was still developing. They believed, but their belief had not yet become stable. Recognizing the limitation of their faith, Jesus addressed them directly:

> *"Wherefore, if God so clothed the grass of the*
> *field...shall he not clothe you, O ye of little faith?"*
> (Matthew 6:30)

This was not a rebuke of absence, but of limitation. Their faith was present, but it had not yet matured into alignment.
> *(See Appendix B — Scriptural Alignment)*

MOSES — BELIEF IN DEVELOPMENT

The theme of developing belief is evident long before the disciples. Moses, called by God at the burning bush, demonstrated the same pattern — initial weakness giving way to growing conviction.

God revealed Himself as the God of Abraham, the God of Isaac, and the God of Jacob. He told Moses He would send him to deliver the children of Israel out of Egypt. Moses responded not with confidence but with doubt.

> *"...Who am I, that I should go unto Pharaoh, and that I should bring forth the children of Israel out of Egypt?"*
>
> (Exodus 3:11)

God answered:

> *"...Certainly I will be with thee..."*
>
> (Exodus 3:12)

Moses pressed further:

> *"...But behold, they will not believe me, nor hearken unto my voice: for they will say, The LORD hath not appeared unto thee."*
>
> (Exodus 4:1)

God responded with demonstration — the rod became a serpent and returned to a rod again:

> *"That they may believe that the LORD God of their fathers... hath appeared unto thee..."*
>
> (Exodus 4:5-9)

Still Moses resisted:

> *"...O my Lord, I am not eloquent... I am slow of speech, and of a slow tongue."*
>
> (Exodus 4:10)

And again:

> *"...O my Lord, send, I pray thee, by the hand of him whom thou wilt send. And the anger of the LORD was kindled against Moses..."*
>
> (Exodus 4:13–14)

God did not abandon him. He appointed Aaron as Moses' spokesman and continued to speak through him. Over time Moses grew. What began as reluctance became resolve. What began as weak belief became demonstrated faith. The man who questioned whether he could stand before Pharaoh would eventually lead a nation through the wilderness.

Thomas walked with Jesus. He witnessed what others only heard about. Yet when the disciples declared that Jesus had risen, their testimony was not enough. He required visual proof before he would believe.

Jesus met him where he was — and then called him higher:

> *"Jesus saith unto him, Thomas, because thou hast seen me, thou hast believed: blessed are they that have not seen, and yet have believed."*
>
> (John 20:29)

This is the pattern. Believing does not always begin in strength. It begins in response — and grows through it.

WHEN PRESENCE IS NOT ENOUGH

When the storm arose, fear overtook the disciples. Despite Jesus' presence, they questioned His provision. Jesus addressed their response directly:

"Why are ye fearful, O ye of little faith?"
(Matthew 8:26)

The issue was not the storm — it was their faith. They saw His power, yet they did not rest in it. This reveals something critical:

Faith is not proven in what is seen, but in how one responds when what is seen is challenged.

FAITH OUTSIDE COVENANT

There were those who understood without proximity. A Roman centurion approached Jesus seeking healing for his servant — not from within His presence, but with understanding. He did not ask for proximity, but authority:

"...I am not worthy that thou shouldest come under my roof: but speak the word only, and my servant shall be healed."
(Matthew 8:8)

He understood that true authority did not require physical presence. Jesus responded with something He had not yet expressed toward His disciples. He said:

"...I have not found so great faith, no, not in Israel."
(Matthew 8:10)

This faith was not rooted in proximity but in understanding and alignment. Jesus said His disciples were of little faith, yet here, He encountered a man whose faith exceeded what He had seen among them. The centurion did not walk with Jesus, but he was aligned with what Jesus represented.

A woman from Canaan came to Jesus, seeking deliverance for her daughter, who was tormented by a demon. Jesus responded:

> *"...I am not sent but unto the lost sheep of the house of Israel."*
>
> (Matthew 15:24)

God's word was written for His people. Jesus said, "I came for the lost sheep of Israel" — He was not just responding to the Canaanite woman's request, He was speaking to a broader issue. He was there for His people.

She was not of Israel. She was not within covenant by lineage. She was not the reason He was sent. Yet she remained. Even in denial, she persisted. She responded, not in anger, but with humility and understanding.

> *"...Truth, Lord: yet the dogs eat of the crumbs which fall from their masters' table."*
>
> (Matthew 15:27)

She did not resist Him or run away; she aligned herself with Him. Jesus responded to her persistence with affirmation:

> *"...O woman, great is thy faith: be it unto the even as thou wilt..."*
>
> (Matthew 15:28)

Her faith was revealed through response. Like the centurion, the Canaanite woman stood outside of covenant and lineage yet demonstrated a level of faith that exceeded those within it. They were not waiting for a Messiah. They were not formed by the same expectation as the disciples, yet when Jesus spoke, they received His words as truth, without resistance. They did not require proximity or repeated demonstration. They believed on Him.

Faith is not established by position or proximity. Those who were expected to recognize Him struggled to fully trust Him. Those who were not expected received Him without hesitation. In doing so, they operated at a level of belief the disciples had not yet reached.

THE PATH TO HIM

Jesus is the way to the Father:

> *"Jesus saith unto him, I am the way, the truth, and the life: no man cometh unto the Father, but by me."*
>
> (John 14:6)

Those from the lost sheep of Israel were called to *believe* and *receive* — the kingdom was announced to them as covenant heirs:

> *"Who are Israelites; to whom pertaineth the adoption, and the glory, and the covenants, and the giving of the law, and the service of God, and the promises."*
>
> (Romans 9:4)
> (See also Matthew 15:24; Matthew 10:6–7; James 1:1)

Others are called to *confess* and *believe* — brought near by mercy into what had already been established:

> *"Wherefore remember, that ye being in time past Gentiles in the flesh, who are called Uncircumcision by that which is called the*

Circumcision in the flesh made by hands; That at that time ye were without Christ, being aliens from the commonwealth of Israel, and strangers from the covenants of promise, having no hope, and without God in the world: But now in Christ Jesus ye who sometimes were far off are made nigh by the blood of Christ."

(Ephesians 2:11-13)

(See also Matthew 15:27–28; Romans 10:9–10)

This is the distinction. One is being drawn in. The other is being developed. This emphasizes difference of covenant position, not difference of worth.

THE INSTABILITY OF PARTIAL FAITH

Peter stepped onto the water. He walked. Then he doubted. The same man who moved in faith was overtaken by fear. Jesus confronted the instability of Peter's fear:

"...O thou of little faith, wherefore didst thou doubt?"

(Matthew 14:31)

The issue was not that Peter did not have faith, but that his faith was unstable.

Peter's encounter in the midst of the storm reveals the tension between believing in Jesus and believing on Him. Peter saw Jesus walking on the water and, believing in Him, said, "Lord, if it be thou, bid me come unto thee on the water." (Matthew 14:28) Jesus answered, "Come." (Matthew 14:29)

Peter stepped out. He walked. In that moment, he was not merely believing in Jesus, he was believing on Him. His focus was fixed; his trust was complete, and he moved in what he believed. As the wind intensified, his attention shifted; what he had been fixed upon was replaced by what surrounded him. Peter began to sink. He cried: "Lord, save me." (Matthew 14:30)

Jesus responded to Peter's doubt with a question:

> *"...O thou of little faith, wherefore didst thou doubt?"*
>
> (Matthew 14:31)

This is the condition of developing faith: It begins in belief but is interrupted by perception. Peter did not stop believing in Jesus. He still knew who Jesus was; he still called on Him for help, but he ceased believing on Him. His faith was overtaken by what he saw.

(See Appendix B — Progression Model)

WHEN FAITH OVERRIDES SIGHT

Naturally, Peter's response is understandable, but this was not a natural moment; it was a spiritual encounter requiring spiritual alignment. Scripture explains this conflict clearly:

> *"But the natural man receiveth not the things of the Spirit of God: for they are foolishness unto him: neither can he know them, because they are spiritually discerned."*
>
> (1 Corinthians 2:14)

What required spiritual alignment was interpreted through natural perception.

As long as Peter's mind remained on Jesus, he walked in peace. When his focus shifted to his circumstances, doubt entered. This is where the transition occurred: From believing on, to merely believing in. From alignment to reaction. He began to sink.

"Thou wilt keep him in perfect peace, whose mind
is stayed on thee: because he trusteth in thee."
(Isaiah 26:3)

Faith that is dependent on what is seen cannot remain when what is seen changes. Peter's faith was present, but it was not yet stable. It moved with his focus, and what moved his focus determined his outcome.

"For we walk by faith, not by sight:"
(2 Corinthians 5:7)

The disciples believed in Him, but they had not yet learned to believe on Him. Their faith was present, but it was not yet established. It responded to what was visible but struggled against what was unseen. This is why Jesus addressed not their actions, but their faith. The issue was not circumstance. It was stability.

There is a difference between belief that reacts and belief that governs — between following what is observed and standing on what is revealed. The disciples were not without faith; they were in development.

Faith, then, is not static. It develops. What begins as acknowledgment must become conviction. What is received must be formed, and what is formed must be lived.

The disciples did not remain in limitation. What they first struggled to trust, they would later embody. What once wavered would become established.

This is the progression, not from absence to
presence, but from presence to maturity.

CHAPTER 11 — THE RENEWAL OF THE MIND

Be not conformed to this world: but be ye
transformed by the renewing of your mind…

(Romans 12:2)

The renewal of the mind refers to ascending levels of awareness that align with developing stages of belief — moving from believing in to believing on, toward the establishment of a belief system, and culminating in the operation of faith. This development requires intentional alignment with truth.

These progressions extend beyond natural perception — moving from what is heard to what is understood, and from what is understood to what governs. The progression established in the previous chapter continues here. Two distinct expressions of belief determine two distinct levels of engagement:

To believe in is to accept what is spoken as true.
To believe on is to place confidence in what you believe is true.

The Word of God instructs us not to be bound by the restrictions we associate with the flesh or with limited understanding. We are not called to conform to this age, nor to remain within the boundaries of what is familiar, but to be transformed — renewed in mind, perception, and understanding, so that we may discern what is excellent, well-pleasing, and aligned with the will of God. As Paul declared, we are called not to conform but to be transformed.

This conversion is not external, but internal. It is the renewing of perception, learning to see, to know, and to understand according to the will of God. As belief strengthens, understanding develops in stages. What is first accepted becomes perceived. What is perceived becomes discerned. What is discerned begins to govern. Each stage reflects a deeper level of awareness, formed not by accumulation of knowledge, but by alignment with truth.

BELIEF AND PROGRESSION

Accessing distinct levels of awareness is common. What is often difficult is recognizing it as it occurs. At times, what appears extraordinary is simply the result of focused belief operating at a higher level of conviction.

It can be approached through various means, including prayer, meditation, and other methods that heighten focus and control.

Human achievement provides many examples. Endurance athletes have completed extreme challenges such as multi-day Iron Man distance competitions across multiple terrains. Individuals have performed feats that assess the limits of the body by withstanding intense conditions, breaking physical thresholds, and sustaining effort beyond what is commonly perceived as possible.

This is often described as "mind over matter" — the ability to push beyond perceived limitations through concentration, discipline, and belief.

These demonstrations suggest that the human capacity extends beyond what is typically exercised. But there is a distinction. What is often described as mind over matter is different from alignment with truth. One draws from self-discipline, will, and internal control. The other flows from relationship — belief rooted in God and dependence on Him.

The difference may seem subtle, but in reality, the contrast is foundational. One is a total reliance on one's own ability, or on systems influenced by the god of this world. The other is a total reliance on The Father recognizing all strength, capacity, and increase come from Him.

This is where belief becomes essential. Belief begins as thought; thought forms understanding; understanding establishes conviction; and conviction, when acted upon consistently, becomes faith.

As belief deepens, so does awareness. What is first heard becomes understood, what is understood becomes discerned, and what is discerned begins to govern. This is progression. The disciples moved through these stages. What they first heard, they later understood. What they understood, they eventually operated in.

Faith is not separate from belief. Faith is belief established through alignment.

TWO SOURCES OF POWER

Everyone serves something — whether deity, person, or desire. This is not a matter of preference, but of reality. Whether one aligns with The Most High, the god of this world, or something influenced by it — the outcome remains the same: service is inevitable. This is why the first commandment is given:

> *"You shall have no other gods before me."*
>
> (Exodus 20:3)

God's desire is that all would come into the knowledge of truth and the redeeming quality found in Jesus Christ. The principles of belief remain constant, but the object of belief determines the outcome. There are two sources: One rooted in The Most High. The other rooted in the god of this world. The distinction is not found in ability, but in source.

THE LIMITS OF IMITATION

Exodus 7 places the two sources in direct confrontation.

> *"And Moses and Aaron went in unto Pharaoh, and they did as the LORD had commanded: and Aaron cast down his rod... and it became a serpent. Then Pharaoh also called the wise men and the sorcerers... and they also did in like manner... but Aaron's rod swallowed up their rods."*
>
> (Exodus 7:10–12)

Aaron's rod became a serpent and consumed the rods of the sorcerers. This revealed a boundary. The magicians were able to imitate, but they could not overcome. What God produced consumed what was imitated. Scripture names the source of that imitation directly:

> *"But if our gospel be hid, it is hid to them that are lost: In whom the god of this world hath blinded the minds of them which believe not..."*
>
> (2 Corinthians 4:3–4)

The enemy does not primarily operate by altering what is seen, but by distorting how it is perceived. Blinding the eyes produces physical limitation; blinding the mind produces spiritual confusion. The mind is the place of decision. When perception is altered, truth becomes obscured. This is how deception is sustained. Those who are not in covenant with The Most High are more susceptible to this influence, not because they lack ability, but because they lack alignment with truth. Job's account establishes the boundary plainly:

> *"And the LORD said unto Satan, Behold, all that*
> *he hath is in thy power; only upon himself put not*
> *forth thine hand..."*

(Job 1:12)

Satan moves within the earth, but he does not operate without boundary. He does not act independently of God's allowance. He does not possess unrestricted authority. Even in affliction, his reach is defined. His influence requires agreement.

There is no compulsion — only consent.

The enemy can manipulate what exists, but he cannot bring something into existence.
He can imitate what is real, but he cannot originate it.

What appears extraordinary is often misunderstood. Some human feats are attributed to "mind over matter," but in many cases, they reflect submission to a system of belief, not true authority. What is being accessed is not creative power, but influence operating within limits.

THE POWER OF ALIGNMENT

> *"I can do all things through Christ which strengtheneth me."*
>
> (Philippians 4:13)

This is not the power of self. It is the power of alignment. The principle holds — belief activates possibility. But alignment determines outcome.

God does not manipulate matter, He created it. He speaks, and things come into existence. He restores what is broken. He heals what is afflicted. He establishes what cannot be sustained by man.

> *"He is above all, and through all, and in you all."*
>
> (Ephesians 4:6)

The enemy operates within limits. God does not. The enemy imitates. God creates. The enemy distorts perception. God reveals truth. Satan's abilities are limited. His influence is temporary. But God is limitless — and those who are aligned with Him are not confined by what appears possible but are strengthened by what is true.

THINK ON THESE THINGS

Paul had deep affection for the church at Philippi. From the beginning of his ministry, they supported him and shared in the work of the Gospel. In his letter, he expresses both gratitude and instruction, urging them not only to follow Christ, but to guard their thoughts.

> *"Finally, brethren, whatsoever things are true, whatsoever things are honest, whatsoever things are just, whatsoever things are pure, whatsoever*

things are lovely, whatsoever things are of good
report; if there be any virtue, and if there be any
praise, think on these things. Those things, which
ye have both learned, and received, and heard, and
seen in me, do: and the God of peace shall be with
you. "

(Philippians 4:8–9)

What we hear, receive, see, and learn shapes how we think. How we think shapes what we believe. What we believe shapes how we live. Thought is not passive; it is formative. It regulates belief, directs conduct, and expresses identity. If our thinking aligns with God, our lives begin to reflect Him. If it does not, we return to ourselves, relying on our own understanding and fulfilling the desires of the flesh.

"For my thoughts are not your thoughts, neither
are your ways my ways, saith the LORD. "

(Isaiah 55:8)

At issue is not God's standard, but our alignment with it. If we are to walk in His ways, our thinking must be transformed and our minds renewed — not conformed to what is familiar but transformed by what is true.

Renewal is not automatic. It must be intentional. God does not simply instruct us to change — He shows us how. We are to be deliberate about what we think. This is the discipline — to reject what distorts, to receive what aligns, and to filter thought through truth rather than through experience alone. Transformation is not only individual, but also collective. We are members of one body, each with distinct functions, but governed by the same Spirit. God does not call His people to isolation; He calls them to alignment.

> *"Now I beseech you, brethren... that ye all speak the same thing... and that there be no divisions among you; but that ye be perfectly joined together in the same mind and in the same judgment."*
>
> (1 Corinthians 1:10)

When a people think together, they move together.

THE POWER OF AGREEMENT

Scripture reveals the power of unified thought:

> *"And the LORD said, Behold, the people is one... and now nothing will be restrained from them, which they have imagined to do."*
>
> (Genesis 11:6)

Unity itself is not inherently righteous — it is the object of that unity that determines its fruit.

> *(See Appendix C — Systems and Perception for how unified systems shape collective understanding.)*

When people operate as one in thought and intention, their capacity increases. But alignment alone is not enough. If unity is rooted in error, it produces destruction. If unity is rooted in truth, it produces power.

ALIGNMENT WITH GOD

God's purpose is not confined to individual transformation — but to the formation of a people. Not divided by culture, language, or background, but united in truth. We are a people formed by God, led by His Spirit, and aligned through His Word. This is how He moves through His people. Not through isolated effort, but through unified alignment.

When thought is disciplined, belief is stabilized. When belief is stabilized, behavior aligns. When behavior aligns, life reflects truth. God orders the steps of those who are aligned with Him, and as alignment deepens, capacity increases.

> *"And it shall come to pass in the last days, saith God, I will pour out of my Spirit upon all flesh: and your sons and your daughters shall prophesy, and your young men shall see visions, and your old men shall dream dreams: And on my servants and on my handmaidens I will pour out in those days of my Spirit..."*
>
> (Acts 2:17–18)

God is not withholding; He is preparing. He is forming a people whose thoughts are aligned, whose minds are renewed, and whose lives reflect His truth.

Think on these things.

CHAPTER 12 — WALKING IN THE SPIRIT: GOVERNED FROM WITHIN

For as many as are led by the Spirit of God, they are the sons of God.

(Romans 8:14)

EQUIPPED FOR ALIGNMENT

Renewed thinking does not develop in isolation. God understood that transformation of the mind requires preparation, and He provided it — appointing specific functions within the body not to replace the Spirit, but to equip His people to receive from Him directly.

> *"And he gave some, apostles; and some, prophets; and some, evangelists; and some, pastors and teachers; For the perfecting of the saints, for the work of the ministry, for the edifying of the body of Christ: Till we all come in the unity of the faith, and of the knowledge of the Son of God..."*

(Ephesians 4:11–13)

These are not figures to be exalted. They are servants appointed for a time and a purpose: Apostles are sent to carry out a mission. Prophets proclaim the will of God. Evangelists preach the Gospel. Pastors guide and teachers instruct.

Their function is not to replace God, but to prepare His people to return to Him. They plant and they water, but God gets the increase. Their role is to equip, to mend what has been disrupted, and to prepare God's children to be led by the Holy Spirit — until all come into unity of faith, until all are fully acquainted with the Son, until maturity is reached, measured not by knowledge alone, but by alignment with Christ.

FROM PRESENCE TO INDWELLING

When Jesus walked the earth, the disciples looked to Him for everything. For truth, for direction, for understanding, and for provision. This was by design. They were being trained to depend on what came from God through Him. But this dependency was not meant to remain external. Jesus said:

> *"And I will pray the Father, and he shall give you another Comforter, that he may abide with you for ever; even the Spirit of truth;... for he dwelleth with you, and shall be in you."*
>
> (John 14:16–17)

And again:

> *"But the Comforter, which is the Holy Ghost, whom the Father will send in my name, he shall teach you all things..."*
>
> (John 14:26)

> *"Howbeit when he, the Spirit of truth, is come, he will guide you into all truth… and he will shew you things to come."*

(John 16:13)

Jesus was preparing them for transition. He was with them, but soon, He would be in them through the Spirit.

THE SPIRIT AS A TEACHER

Jesus did not instruct His disciples to depend on man for truth. He pointed them to the Father.

> *"Believest thou not that I am in the Father, and the Father in me? The words that I speak… I speak not of myself: but the Father that dwelleth in me, he doeth the works."*

(John 14:10)

What Jesus received from the Father, He spoke. What He spoke, He demonstrated. The same pattern continues. The Spirit that dwelled in Him now dwells in God's children. To walk in the Spirit is to live from what is received, not from what is assumed. To be taught from within, not governed solely by what is external.

Apostles, prophets, evangelists, pastors, and teachers do not replace the Spirit. They confirm what the Spirit reveals. They equip God's children to hear, to receive, and to walk accordingly.

Their purpose is not to create dependence, but to prepare for independence in the Spirit.

SUBMISSION AND ALIGNMENT

To walk in the Spirit requires submission.

> *"Submit yourselves therefore to God. Resist the*
> *devil, and he will flee from you."*
>
> (James 4:7)

Submission is not forced but chosen. Submission is the acceptance of one's position within God's order to align with His will, His authority, and His purpose.

> *God calls. God invites. But man must respond.*

The struggle is internal.

> *"For the weapons of our warfare are not carnal,*
> *but mighty through God to the pulling down of*
> *strongholds; Casting down imaginations, and*
> *every high thing that exalteth itself against the*
> *knowledge of God, and bringing into captivity*
> *every thought to the obedience of Christ;"*
>
> (2 Corinthians 10:4–5)

Strongholds are not physical; they are patterns of thought. They are beliefs that oppose truth. They are imaginations that distort what God has revealed. To walk in the Spirit requires discipline of thought. Every idea must be examined. Every imagination must be challenged. Every thought must be brought into alignment.

THE PRACTICE OF RENEWAL

Transformation is practiced, not random. Developed and sustained through intention. There is a process: The discipline begins with recognition — thoughts can be managed, and unchecked thoughts lead to misalignment. It continues with acknowledgment — not every thought is truth. It requires action — every thought must be brought into alignment with Christ, rejecting what opposes Him and receiving what reflects Him. This is the discipline of renewal.

Faith is not instant — it is formed. It begins with belief. It grows through exposure to truth. It matures through alignment. What is heard becomes understood. What is understood becomes conviction. What is lived consistently becomes faith. Faith is the result of alignment sustained over time.

WALKING IN THE SPIRIT

To walk in the Spirit is to live from what God reveals — to think as He instructs, to function as He leads, and to respond as He directs. This journey is not passive; it is intentional. It requires attention, consistency, and surrender.

It produces clarity.
It produces alignment.
It produces life.

WORDS AND ALIGNMENT

Words are not empty. They carry meaning and meaning shapes alignment.

"But I say unto you, That every idle word that men shall speak, they shall give account thereof in the day of judgment."

(Matthew 12:36)

What is spoken reflects what is understood, and what is repeated reinforces what is believed. If something is named incorrectly, it is not without effect. Not because the sound itself holds power, but because what it represents does.

To walk in the Spirit is to speak from what has been revealed — not from what has been inherited, repeated, or assumed. What governs the mind will govern the mouth. What comes from the mouth reveals what has been formed within. This is why renewal matters. Words do not merely reflect alignment — they reinforce it.

CHAPTER 13 — THE HELPMATE: COVENANT AND DESIGN

Nevertheless neither is the man without the woman, neither the woman without the man, in the Lord.

(1 Corinthians 11:11)

To understand the design of marriage, one must first understand the structure of covenant upon which it is built.

THE STRUCTURE OF COVENANT: DIVINE AND MARITAL

Marriage does not imitate covenant loosely—it inherits its structure directly from it.

What God established with His people, He revealed through marriage. The same principles that govern divine covenant are not abstract truths; they are lived realities within the marital union. To understand one is to better understand the other.

CHOSEN WITH INTENTION

God did not enter into covenant with His people casually. He chose them. Not because of their strength, nor their consistency, but because of His will. His covenant began with a deliberate act of choosing — a decision that preceded performance. Marriage follows this same pattern.

A husband and wife do not enter covenant because they feel aligned in every moment, but because they have chosen one another with intention. That choice establishes the foundation upon which everything else is built.

> *As God chooses His people, so a man chooses his wife, and a wife chooses her husband — not for a moment, but for a lifetime.*

Where choice is replaced with convenience, covenant gives way to instability.

DEFINED BY TRUTH

God did not leave His covenant undefined. He established it through truth—commands, expectations, and boundaries that clarified the relationship. His people were not left to determine what faithfulness looked like. It was revealed. Marriage reflects this same order.

It is not sustained by assumption or personal interpretation. It requires clarity — what faithfulness means, what honor requires, what responsibility looks like. Truth defines the structure.

> *As God gives His people instruction to preserve covenant, so must husband and wife live within defined understanding to preserve their union.*

Where truth is absent, confusion enters. Where confusion enters, covenant weakens.

EXCLUSIVE IN DEVOTION

God's covenant demands exclusivity. "You shall have no other gods before Me" (Exodus 20:3) is not a suggestion — it is a boundary. His relationship with His people cannot coexist with divided allegiance. Idolatry is not merely disobedience; it is relational betrayal. Marriage mirrors this reality.

A husband and wife are set apart for one another. There is no allowance for shared intimacy, divided loyalty, or competing affections that threaten the union.

> *As God requires undivided devotion from His people, so marriage requires undivided devotion between husband and wife.*

Adultery is not simply an act — it is a violation of covenant identity, just as idolatry is in the divine relationship.

SEALED THROUGH SACRIFICE

God's covenant was not established without cost. Throughout Scripture, covenant is marked by sacrifice. Sacrifice affirms the seriousness of the bond. It reveals that covenant is not sustained by convenience, but by cost. Marriage carries this same requirement.

It is not maintained through self-preservation, but through self-denial. Each partner is called to lay down preference, pride, and personal control for the sake of the union.

As God demonstrates His covenant through sacrifice, so must husband and wife sustain theirs through continual giving.

ENDURING BEYOND CONDITION

God's covenant does not dissolve when challenged. Though His people falter, His commitment remains. His faithfulness is not reactive; it is rooted in who He is. Covenant, by nature, is designed to endure beyond condition. Marriage reflects this endurance.

It is not held together by ease, nor sustained by favorable seasons. It is built to remain through hardship, misunderstanding, and time.

A relationship that only functions under ideal conditions has not yet become covenant. Yet this endurance must be rightly understood. Covenant does not require the acceptance of harm. God's covenant is never expressed through harm.

He corrects, but He does not destroy. He disciplines, but He does not abuse. His faithfulness does not manifest as oppression, nor does His authority produce harm against those He has bound Himself to.

In the same way, marriage does not require the acceptance of physical, emotional, or psychological abuse. Such actions are not expressions of covenantal hardship—they are violations of covenant itself.

Where harm is inflicted, covenant is not being upheld; it is being broken in practice.

Endurance, therefore, applies to difficulty — not to destruction. It calls for faithfulness through trial, not silence in the presence of harm. To remain committed is not to remain unprotected. To uphold covenant is not to submit to violation.

Just as God's covenant preserves and sustains, so must the marital covenant reflect that same order.

WITNESSED IN ACCOUNTABILITY

God's covenant is not hidden — it is established in the open, with Himself as witness. He declares it. He affirms it. He holds His people accountable to it. Covenant is not private in its responsibility, even if it is personal in its experience. Marriage follows this same pattern.

It is entered into before witnesses — before God, and before others. This establishes accountability. It affirms that what is declared carries weight beyond the individuals themselves.

> *As God stands as witness to His covenant, so He stands as witness to marriage.*

What is witnessed cannot be treated lightly, because it is not only known—it is held to account.

REMEMBERED IN PRACTICE

God does not allow His covenant to fade into memory. He establishes reminders — laws, feasts, signs — so that His people continually return to what was established. Covenant must be remembered actively, not passively. Marriage requires the same discipline.

It is not sustained by a moment in time, but by daily practice. Love must be expressed. Commitment must be reaffirmed. The covenant must be lived, not assumed.

What is not remembered in practice will eventually be forgotten in purpose.

COVENANT CONFIRMED

Marriage is not merely a human institution; it is a living demonstration of divine covenant. It reveals, in visible form, the same principles by which God relates to His people. To weaken marriage is to distort that reflection. To uphold covenant in marriage is to preserve it. For in both, the standard remains the same:

What is chosen must be upheld.
What is defined must be obeyed.
What is exclusive must be guarded.
What is sacrificial must be sustained.
What is enduring must remain.
What is witnessed must be honored.
What is remembered must be lived.

Only then does relationship become covenant.

COVENANT AND ORDER

In God's infinite wisdom, He created man and woman to dwell together. From the beginning, He declared:

> *"It is not good that the man should be alone; I will make him an help meet for him."*
>
> (Genesis 2:18)

He called the woman a help meet — not a servant, not a subordinate in worth, but a companion. An ally. A confidante. One who assists in purpose and participates in covenant.

Within this relationship, God established order. The man is called to love his wife as Christ loves the church. The woman is called to be in subjection to her husband. This has often been misunderstood. Subjection has been interpreted as dominance. Submission has been perceived as diminishing. But a proper understanding reveals something entirely different.

It reveals design.

SUBJECTION AND SUBMISSION

Words carry meaning, but meaning can shift over time. Etymology seeks to recover original intent. To understand submission, we must return to its source. Scripture provides the framework:

> *"Likewise, ye wives, be in subjection to your own husbands; that, if any (husband) obey not the word, they also may ... be won by the conversation of the wives;"*
>
> (1 Peter 3:1)

Here, *conversation* refers to behavior. The principle is clear: a life aligned with righteousness has the power to influence what words alone cannot. But the tension arises around the word subjection. Subjection and submission often evoke images of control, bondage, or loss of identity. Yet in this instance this is not its intended meaning.

SUBMISSION DEFINED

To submit *is to yield or give oneself willingly to the authority of another.*
To be subject *is to be placed under authority of another, either voluntarily or by force.*

This distinction matters. Submission is always voluntary, yet subjection may not be. In covenant, submission is chosen, not imposed. Scripture extends this principle beyond marriage:

> *"Submit yourselves one to another in the fear of God."*
>
> (Ephesians 5:21)

> *"Likewise, ye younger, submit yourselves unto the elder..."*
>
> (1 Peter 5:5)

These are not structures of oppression; they are expressions of order — relational alignment. Each operates within their responsibility while honoring the authority of the other. The word translated as submit and subject is the same in Greek. The word hupotasso. Derived from:

Hupo — under
Tasso — to arrange, appoint, or order.

Together, it expresses: to agree to an appointed position willingly and mutually within an established order, under authority, while retaining responsibility.

The words submit and subject carry weight that modern language often avoids. Their synonyms reveal what is sometimes obscured.

To commit is to entrust — to transfer something into the custody and charge of another, placing trust and responsibility in their hands. To consign is to transfer into the custody of another specifically for preservation and safekeeping. These definitions illuminate what submission truly means in covenant. It is not the surrender of worth. It is the transfer of trust — custody, care, protection, and preservation placed willingly into the order God has established.

Submission, therefore, is not loss. It is entrusting.

Submission defined — To mutually agree to an appointed position under the authority of another, while retaining one's own responsibility and authority, and transferring one's custody and care for safekeeping, protection, guardianship, and preservation.

Submission is the alignment of authority.

SUBMISSION IN COVENANT

To submit is to entrust or commit oneself to one's care, responsibility, and well-being into the order God has established. It is the transfer of trust for preservation, protection, and purpose.

Through salvation, God's children enter into covenant with Him. We submit to His authority by agreement and entrust our lives to Him. In doing so, we receive both identity and responsibility, for preservation, protection, and purpose.

In marriage, this principle is mirrored. A wife's submission is not inferiority — it is participation in order. She willingly aligns herself within the covenant structure recognizing both her authority and her responsibility. The husband, in turn, accepts a charge. Not dominance, but stewardship. Not control, but responsibility. They are equal. He is responsible for her; entrusted with her preservation, protection, and purpose.

Within the Trinity, there is submission, but no inferiority. The Son submits to the Father. The Spirit proceeds according to the will of God. Yet all are coequal. As in marriage, the woman is not less than the man. The man is not greater than the woman.

They are equal in value, yet distinct in function.

THE "WEAKER" VESSEL

Scripture describes the woman as the weaker vessel:

> *"Likewise, ye husbands, dwell with them according to knowledge, giving honour unto the wife, as unto the weaker vessel, and as being heirs together of the grace of life..."*
>
> (1 Peter 3:7)

The Hebrew behind help meet is *ezer kenegdo* — a helper suitable for him, one who corresponds to him. It describes function and fitness, not subordination. She was not made beneath him. She was made for him — distinct in design, equal in worth, and necessary in purpose.

Weaker does not mean inferior. It describes condition, not worth. The Greek word asthenes refers to physical distinction, not spiritual deficiency. Descriptive, not defining. Yet within this distinction is design. Strength, in Scripture, is not only what is possessed, but also what is produced.

The phrase weaker vessel has been taken out of context and used to diminish. Those unfamiliar with Scripture have drawn conclusions from it that Scripture itself does not support. Decisions have been made. Worth has been assigned. Identity has been reduced — all from a misreading of a single phrase.

Description is not definition. Consider the structure of any organized effort. A leader is appointed not always because they are the most skilled, but because the task requires order. Those who support that leader are not lesser — they are essential. When the task changes, the roles may shift. What remains constant is the goal.

This is the pattern of the marital covenant. Order is not permanent hierarchy. It is purposeful structure. The woman is not permanently beneath. She is specifically positioned — for purpose, for contribution, for covenant. The woman contributes to the usefulness of the man through her design.

From the Greek skeuos, vessel refers to an instrument or apparatus designed for a specific purpose — not an object of use, but a necessary component of function.

An apparatus is the equipment or instrument necessary for a particular function used by a technician. In this context, the woman is not incidental; she is essential. She is a necessary component within God's design, contributing to the effectiveness, stability, and purpose of the man.

This is not a statement of hierarchy, but of function. A technician possesses a specialized skill, trained, precise, and necessary for a specific outcome. In the same way, the woman carries a capacity uniquely her own. She contributes in ways that cannot be replicated, fulfilling a role that is distinct, intentional, and designed by God.

The word apparatus is not used to define the woman as an object, but to reveal the depth of her significance. She is not an item — she is a force.

She must understand her worth to God and the significance of her position to the man. His recognition does not establish it. God already has. When that awareness is carried into union by both, it determines how far they journey together.

"Whoso findeth a wife findeth a good thing, and obtaineth favour of the LORD."

(Proverbs 18:22)

When a man finds a wife, he does not merely find companionship — he finds alignment. He finds one equipped to contribute to his purpose, to strengthen his function, and to participate in covenant with him.

Within this description is deeper meaning. The woman's design includes strengthening — there is strength in her design. She supports, upholds, and establishes. She is not lesser, but essential. Her worth is not assigned by circumstance but established by design.

These qualities are not limited to women in marriage; they apply to all women. A woman's strength, purpose, and worth are undeniable. Her design is not dependent on her role. It is inherent to her identity.

STRENGTH IN DESIGN

The concept of sthenos speaks to strength. The concept of histēmi speaks to establishing — to cause to stand, to set in place, to make firm. So, it is here.

The woman's role is not defined by lack,
but by contribution.

She strengthens.
She establishes.
She sustains.

She contributes to the man's ability to stand, to remain steady, to remain aligned, and to remain intact within covenant — supporting him, upholding him, standing with him, reinforcing his ability to endure, to remain firm, to continue in purpose — steady, present, and aligned. She contributes to the stability of the man and the integrity of the family.

It is intentional.
It is consistent.
It is necessary.

RESPONSIBILITY OF THE HUSBAND

"Likewise, ye husbands, dwell with them according to knowledge, giving honour unto the wife, as unto the weaker vessel, and as being heirs together of the grace of life; that your prayers be not hindered."

(1 Peter 3:7)

This instruction is not casual; it is precise. To dwell is to live together in unity. To act with knowledge is to operate in truth and understanding. To give honor is to assign value of the highest degree.

The husband is called to live with his wife in understanding, recognizing her as essential; one who strengthens, supports, and sustains both him and the family within God's design.

She is not incidental — she is integral. Not inferior—but aligned. They are heirs together of the grace of life. How he treats her directly affects his standing before God:

"...that your prayers be not hindered."

(1 Peter 3:7)

His responsibility is weighty — his treatment of his wife affects his relationship with God. How he leads determines what he receives.

LEADERSHIP AND RELATIONSHIP

Leadership is not domination. To lead is not to control. God gave man dominion over creation, not over one another. Authority in relationship is expressed through care, through honor, through responsibility. Not through force.

Marriage is not a hierarchy of worth. Marriage is a structure of order. A mutual agreement to function within God's design. Each fulfilling their role. Each honoring the other. Each contributing to the whole.

When order is understood, submission becomes alignment, leadership becomes responsibility, relationship becomes covenant, and the result is stability.

THE CALL TO UNITY

Scripture concludes with this charge:

> *"Finally, be ye all of one mind, having compassion one of another, love as brethren, be pitiful, be courteous: Not rendering evil for evil, or railing for railing: but contrariwise blessing; knowing that ye are thereunto called, that ye should inherit a blessing."*
>
> (1 Peter 3:8–9)

This is the model. Not domination, but unity. Not control, but care. Not division, but alignment. This is not a human standard — it is a divine one. Where it is lived, covenant is not merely practiced. It is reflected.

FINAL REFLECTION

What has been revealed must now be responded to. This work was not presented as information to be considered, but as truth to be examined.

Not everything that has been accepted is aligned.
Not everything that is familiar is true.
Not everything that has been practiced was established by God.

The responsibility, therefore, is not to agree but to discern. Recognition alone is not enough. What is revealed must be answered. There will always be tension between what has been lived and what is being revealed, between what feels familiar and what is true, and between what has been accepted and what must now be examined.

This conflict is not a contradiction; it is an invitation. An invitation to return. Not to what has been practiced — but to what was established.

This return requires separation. It requires surrender. It requires alignment. What has been carried must be released. What has been replaced must be restored.

That truth received by revelation is categorically different from truth received by tradition or teaching — it is the foundation upon which God is rebuilding His relationship with His people.

This distinction is not minor. It is the difference between a people who know about God and a people who know Him. It is the difference between a faith inherited and a faith received. Between a religion practiced and a relationship lived.

Peter did not arrive at his confession through the accumulated wisdom of those around him. He did not reason his way to it. He did not inherit it from his fathers. The Father revealed it — directly, personally, and unmistakably. And in that moment, Peter was no longer merely a follower. He became a receiver.

This is what the remnant carries. Not a better tradition. Not a more refined system. But direct reception from the Father — the same access Peter demonstrated, now made available through the indwelling of the Holy Spirit.

The church was never meant to be built on what man could construct. It was meant to be built on what only God could reveal. Where that revelation is absent, what remains is structure without foundation — familiar in form, but empty of the life that only comes from above.

This is the new beginning. Not new in origin but restored in practice. A return to what was always intended — that His people would hear His voice, receive His truth, and walk in alignment with what He alone reveals.

The question is no longer what has been revealed. The question is what will be done with it. Truth does not adjust to accommodate us. We are called to align with it, and alignment requires movement. Not toward what is comfortable, but toward what is true.

The remnant is not identified by knowledge; they are revealed by response. They are those who hear and return, who see and realign, who recognize and move. Not because it is easy, but because it is necessary.

This is the call.

To remain.
To discern.
To endure.
And to return to what has always been.

APPENDIX A — MISINTERPRETATION AND SUBSTITUTION

The following study supports the discussion of misinterpretation, tradition, and substitution developed throughout the manuscript — particularly in Chapter 4 on the Law, Chapter 5 on the illusion of freedom, and Chapter 6 on the normalization of substitution.

THE NATURE OF MISINTERPRETATION

This is how substitution occurs — not by removing truth, but by redefining it.

A single passage isolated from its context can appear to contradict what was clearly established. When interpretation replaces alignment, confusion follows.

When something opposes what has already been spoken, it is not truth that has shifted — it is understanding that has been misapplied.

HOW SUBSTITUTION OCCURS

Truth is rarely discarded outright. It is not often attacked directly. Instead it is displaced. Something else is introduced as an alternative. It appears reasonable. It appears beneficial. It appears harmless. And over time it assumes the place of what was originally established.

> *This is the pattern — not destruction, but substitution.*

God is not denied; He is repositioned. Truth is not rejected; it is reinterpreted. What was once clear becomes obscured — not because it has changed, but because something else has taken its place.

THE ROLE OF TRADITION

Tradition sustains itself through repetition. It is inherited, practiced, and normalized — often without ever being questioned. Over time what is practiced begins to define what is believed, and what is believed — if not assessed — can drift from the truth it once reflected.

The Bible warns that tradition can render the Word of God ineffective. The issue is not tradition itself, but the authority it is given. When practices passed down through generations are accepted without examination, they can move beyond expression and become substitution — replacing what was revealed with what has merely been repeated.

WHEN REPLACEMENT BECOMES STANDARD

Eventually what was once true is no longer recognized — not because it has changed, but because something else has taken its place.

THE REQUIREMENT OF DISCERNMENT

Not everything that is read is rightly divided. Not everything that is taught is aligned.

The Holy Spirit does not affirm what is merely familiar. He reveals what is true. He searches, instructs, corrects, and brings into remembrance what has been spoken by God.

Where tradition repeats, the Spirit reveals.
Where man asserts, the Spirit discerns.
Where substitution has occurred, the Spirit restores.

SCRIPTURAL ANCHORS

"Making the word of God of none effect through your tradition, which ye have delivered: and many such like things ye do."

(Mark 7:13)

"Beware lest any man spoil you through philosophy and vain deceit, after the tradition of men, after the rudiments of the world, and not after Christ."

(Colossians 2:8)

"Study to shew thyself approved unto God, a workman that needeth not to be ashamed, rightly dividing the word of truth."

(2 Timothy 2:15)

Misinterpretation does not require intention. It requires only exposure without examination. What is received without discernment can be accepted without alignment. And what is accepted without alignment can govern without correction.

This is why every believer is called not merely to read but to rightly divide. Not merely to receive but to examine. Not merely to practice but to align.

Truth has not been lost. It has been replaced.

And what has been replaced can be restored — through the Spirit, through the Word, and through the willingness to return to what was established.

Note on Sources: All Scripture citations from the King James Version unless otherwise noted. Cross references: Chapter 5 — The Law: Instruction to Fulfillment, Chapter 6 — The Illusion of Freedom, Chapter 7 — The Pattern of Substitution.

APPENDIX B — BELIEF, FAITH, AND UNDERSTANDING

The following word study supports the progression of belief, faith, and understanding discussed in Chapter 10, and the significance of Peter's name in Chapter 9.

Belief begins with acceptance. It is the acknowledgment that something is true. Belief develops into conviction. It becomes a principle — something held, not just heard. Faith is the expression of that conviction. It is belief lived — demonstrated through trust, alignment, and action.

Faith is born out of belief. Where belief is absent, faith cannot exist.

GREEK WORD STUDY

Believe — pisteuō (4100): to think to be true, to be persuaded of, to place confidence in.
Faith — pistis (4102): conviction of truth; belief accompanied by trust and confidence.

133

> **Root** — peitho (3982): to persuade, to induce belief, to
> produce inward certainty.

Both pisteuō and pistis originate from peitho. Yet persuasion alone does not produce trust. To believe is the entry point — the acceptance of a declaration as true. Faith is conviction — belief that has been tested, established, and accompanied by trust. The difference between them is not one of kind but of depth. One is the seed. The other is the fruit.

> *"So then belief comes by hearing, and hearing by the Word of God."*
>
> (Romaiym 10:17, Eth Cepher)

> *(Strong's Concordance reference numbers are provided for readers who wish to study the original language further.)*

HEBREW UNDERSTANDING

> **Believe** — leh-ah-meen: to accept or deem something true.
> **Belief** — emunah: deeper conviction, devotion, and consecration.
> **Faith** — emunah: steadfast and unwavering trust, confidence, and loyalty.

The Hebrew reveals that belief and faith share the same word — emunah. This is intentional. They are not two separate destinations but two expressions of the same devotion at different levels of maturity. What the Greek identifies through precision, the Hebrew expresses through devotion.

To believe is inward acceptance. Belief is established devotion. Faith is security and action rooted in that devotion.

"But without belief it is impossible to please him: for he that comes to God must believe that he is and he is a rewarder of them that diligently seek him."

(Ivriym 11:6, Eth Cepher)

(Strong's Concordance reference numbers are provided for readers who wish to study the original language further.)

PROGRESSION MODEL

Believe — Entry (acceptance)
Belief — Stabilization (conviction)
Faith — Demonstration (action)

To believe → to form a belief → to walk in faith

They are not identical; they are progressive. Each represents a higher level of conscious alignment.

SCRIPTURAL ALIGNMENT

Mark 9:23 — Belief activates possibility.
Romans 10:10 — Belief leads to righteousness.
Hebrews 11:1 — Faith/Belief is substance.

Substance — assurance
Hope — anticipating with expectation
Evidence — conviction and confidence

TEXTUAL OBSERVATION

Romans 10:9–16 uses the word believe six times as its primary focus. The Eth Cepher renders verse 17 as:

> *"So then belief comes by hearing, and hearing by the Word of God."*

This suggests greater consistency with the passage's emphasis on believing rather than faith. One word does not belong in this passage if belief and faith carry different meanings.

> *So then faith cometh by hearing, and hearing by the word of God.*
>
> (Romans 10:17, KJV)

> *So then belief comes by hearing, and hearing by the Word of Yahuah.*
>
> (Romaiym 10:17, Eth Cepher)

Hebrews 11:1 — KJV reads: Now faith is the substance of things hoped for, the evidence of things not seen. Eth Cepher reads: Now belief is the substance of things hoped for, the evidence of things not seen. The substitution of belief for faith throughout Hebrews 11 suggests the chapter is describing an established system of devotion demonstrated through action — consistent with the progression from believing to belief to faith developed in this study.

DEUTERONOMY 32:20— FAITH OR BELIEF

In Deuteronomy 32, the children of Israel are described as having corrupted themselves — a perverse and crooked generation who forsook God, lightly esteemed the Rock of their salvation, provoked Him to jealousy with strange gods, and sacrificed unto devils. This was not a people struggling with active trust. This was a people who had lost their devotion entirely. Against that context the two translations reveal a meaningful distinction:

> *"And he said, I will hide my face from them, I will see what their end shall be: for they are a very froward generation, children in whom is no faith."*
>
> (Deuteronomy 32:20, KJV)

> *"And he said, I will hide my face from them, I will see what their end shall be: for they are a very froward generation, children in whom is no belief."*
>
> (Devariym 32:20, Eth Cepher)

Would God look for active trust — faith — in a people who had abandoned their devotion to Him entirely? Or would He identify the absence of something more foundational — belief, defined as profound dedication and consecration? Paul confirms in Romans that God's response to Israel was rooted in their unbelief — not their lack of active trust:

> *"Well; because of unbelief they were broken off."*
>
> (Romans 11:20)

The condition God identified in Deuteronomy 32:20 was not the failure of active trust. It was the collapse of devotion. And where devotion collapses, active trust has nothing left to stand on. The Eth Cepher rendering — no belief — is therefore more consistent with both the context of Deuteronomy 32 and Paul's later confirmation in Romans 11.

HEBREWS 11 — BELIEF IN ACTION

The following passage from the Eth Cepher demonstrates the progression established in this appendix. Each verse is presented first as rendered in the Eth Cepher, followed by an interpretive reading with the full definition of belief inserted in place of the word itself. This allows the reader to see not merely what belief means — but what belief produces.

> *"Now belief is the substance of things hoped for, the evidence of things not seen."*
> (Ivriym 11:1, Eth Cepher)

Now, a habit of mind that has developed into a principled system of belief and devotion is the substance of things hoped for, the evidence of things not seen.

> *"For by it the elders obtained a good report."*
> (Ivriym 11:2, Eth Cepher)

> *"Through belief we understand that the worlds are framed by the Word of God, so that things which are seen were not made of things which do appear."*
> (Ivriym 11:3, Eth Cepher)

Through a habit of mind that has developed into a principled system of belief and devotion, we understand that the worlds are framed by the Word of God, so that things which are seen were not made of things which do appear.

> *"By belief Abel offered unto God a more excellent sacrifice than Cain, by which he obtained witness that he was righteous, God testifying of his gifts: and by it he being dead yet speaks."*
> (Ivriym 11:4, Eth Cepher)

By a habit of mind that has developed into a principled system of belief and devotion, Abel offered unto Yahuah a more excellent sacrifice than Cain, by which he obtained witness that he was righteous, God testifying of his gifts: and by it he being dead yet speaks.

> *"By belief Enoch was translated that he should not see death; and was not found, because God had translated him: for before his translation he had his testimony, that he pleased God."*
>
> (Ivriym 11:5, Eth Cepher)

By a habit of mind that has developed into a principled system of belief and devotion, Enoch was translated that he should not see death; and was not found, because God had translated him: for before his translation he had his testimony, that he pleased God.

> *"But without belief it is impossible to please him: for he that comes to God must believe that he is and he is a rewarder of them that diligently seek him."*
>
> (Ivriym 11:6, Eth Cepher)

But without a habit of mind that has developed into a principled system of belief and devotion, it is impossible to please him: for he that comes to God must believe that he is and he is a rewarder of them that diligently seek him.

One must first believe in order to have belief.

*"By belief Noah, being warned of God of things
not seen as yet, moved with fear, prepared an ark
to the saving of his house; by the which he
condemned the world, and became heir of the
righteousness which is by belief."*
(Ivriym 11:7, Eth Cepher)

By a habit of mind that has developed into a principled system
of belief and devotion, Noah, being warned of God of things not
seen as yet, moved with fear, prepared an ark to the saving of his
house; by the which he condemned the world, and became heir
of the righteousness which is by a habit of mind that has
developed into a principled system of belief and devotion.

*"By belief Abraham, when he was called to go out
into a place which he should after receive for an
inheritance, obeyed; and he went out, not knowing
whither he went."*
(Ivriym 11:8, Eth Cepher)

By a habit of mind that has developed into a principled system
of belief and devotion, Abraham, when he was called to go into
a place which he should after receive for an inheritance, obeyed;
and he went out, not knowing whither he went.

*"By belief he sojourned in the land of promise, as
in a strange country, dwelling in tabernacles with
Isaac and Jacob, the heirs with him of the same
promise."*
(Ivriym 11:9, Eth Cepher)

By a habit of mind that has developed into a principled system
of belief and devotion, he sojourned in the land of promise, as in

a strange country, dwelling in tabernacles with Isaac and Jacob, the heirs with him of the same promise.

> *"For he looked for a city which has foundations, whose Builder and Maker is God."*
>
> (Ivriym 11:10, Eth Cepher)

> *"Through belief also Sarah herself received strength to conceive seed, and was delivered of a child when she was past age, because she judged him faithful who had promised."*
>
> (Ivriym 11:11, Eth Cepher)

Through a habit of mind that has developed into a principled system of belief and devotion, Sarah herself received strength to conceive seed, and was delivered of a child when she was past age, because she judged him faithful who had promised.

CLOSING DECLARATION

To believe is the conscious acceptance of a statement as truth. A belief is a mindset that has developed into a system of principles and devotion.
Faith is a disciplined way of living that involves unwavering allegiance, loyalty, and complete trust.

LEXICAL STUDY — SIMON, PETER, ROCK, AND CEPHAS

This study supports the discussion of Peter's revelation in Chapter 9 and the significance of the name given to him by Christ.

Simon — Hebrew/Greek — Heard; one who listens with attention and intent.
Peter (Petros) — Greek — Rock or stone.
Rock (Petra) — Greek — Large rock; foundation.
Cephas (Kephas) — Aramaic — Stone.

The Rock upon which Christ builds His church is not the man but the revelation. One that cannot be constructed — only received. Peter's name reflects his transformation: from one who hears to one who receives."

Note on Sources: Greek definitions drawn from Strong's Exhaustive Concordance. Hebrew definitions drawn from Strong's Exhaustive Concordance and the Eth Cepher. Webster's definitions consulted for English clarification.

APPENDIX C — TIME, SYSTEMS, AND INTERPRETATION

The following study supports the discussion of time, naming, and systems developed in Chapter 7, and the argument about how human structures have shaped perception and displaced what God originally established.

Time is not only measured but also interpreted. What is observed in creation is often reordered through systems established by man. Over time these systems become standard, and what was once natural becomes structured according to human design. When time is altered, understanding is altered, and when understanding is altered, alignment is disrupted.

> *"And he shall speak great words against the Most High… and think to change times and laws…"*
>
> (Daniel 7:25)

The names of the days of the week reflect the influence of pagan systems on what was once ordered by God. What God established was identified through function and order. What man introduced was named through mythology and cultural practice.

(See Chapter 7 — Systems of Men)

CALENDAR SYSTEMS

Biblical — Lunar-solar — Based on signs and seasons established by God.
Roman — Solar — Civil structure introduced by human governance.
Gregorian — Solar — Current global standard.

Daylight Saving — Adjusted — Alters perceived time within established systems.

DAYS OF THE WEEK

Sunday — Old English — Sun
Monday — Old English — Moon
Tuesday — Norse — Tyr
Wednesday — Norse — Odin
Thursday — Norse — Thor
Friday — Norse — Freyja
Saturday — Latin — Saturn

Not one of the seven days carries a name rooted in the order God established. Each reflects the influence of systems that replaced what was originally observed.

The naming of days is one expression of a broader pattern — systems of governance, religion, culture, and time have all functioned as frameworks through which perception is shaped.

SYSTEMS AND PERCEPTION

Political — Governance — Produces dependence on human authority.
Religious — Doctrine — Produces structured interpretation replacing direct revelation.
Cultural — Norms — Produces normalized behavior accepted without examination.
Time — Measurement — Produces shaped perception of what is observed.

INTERPRETIVE IMPACT

Altered time — Misaligned practice.
Repetition — Normalized error.
System reliance — Displaced truth.
Substitution — What was revealed replaced by what was repeated.

What is practiced long enough becomes established. What is established is rarely questioned. And what is rarely questioned begins to define what is believed.

This is not only the pattern of tradition. It is the pattern of systems. When perception is shaped by what man has introduced rather than what God established, alignment becomes difficult — not because truth has changed, but because the framework through which it is received has been altered. The instruction remains:

"Remember the Sabbath day, to keep it holy."
(Exodus 20:8)

*Note on Sources: Calendar and day name origins drawn from standard
etymological records including the Oxford English Dictionary and historical
studies of the Julian and Gregorian calendar systems. Calendar system
histories drawn from standard historical records of Roman and ecclesiastical
calendar reform. Daniel 7:25 and Exodus 20:8 cited from the King James
Version.*

REFERENCES

The Holy Bible, King James Version. (1769). Cambridge
    Edition.

Cepher Publishing Group, LLC. (2018). Eth Cepher. Retrieved
    from https://www.cepher.net/is-the-cepher-a-direct-
    translation.aspx

IELTS Australia. (n.d.). Grammar 101: Belief vs. Believe.
    Retrieved from https://ielts.com.au/articles/grammar-
    101-belief-vs-believe/

Merck Manuals. (n.d.). Placebos. Retrieved from
    https://www.merckmanuals.com/home/drugs/overview-
    of-drugs/placebos

Strong, James, S.T.D., L.D. (2019). Strong's Exhaustive
    Concordance of the Bible. e-Sword Digital Edition.

Webster's Dictionary 1828. (n.d.). Belief. Retrieved from
    http://webstersdictionary1828.com/Dictionary/belief

Webster's Dictionary 1828. (n.d.). Faith. Retrieved from
    http://webstersdictionary1828.com/Dictionary/faith

www.ingramcontent.com/pod-product-compliance
Lightning Source LLC
Chambersburg PA
CBHW061428160726
47995CB00003B/795